THE IMPOVERISHMENT OF NATIONS

THE IMPOVERISHMENT OF NATIONS

THE ISSUES FACING THE GLOBAL ECONOMY

Leigh Skene

PROFILE BOOKS

First published in Great Britain in 2009 by
Profile Books Ltd
3A Exmouth House
Pine Street
London EC1R OJH
www.profilebooks.com

Typeset in Times by MacGuru Ltd
info@macguru.org.uk
Printed and bound in Britain by
Bell & Bain Ltd

A CIP catalogue record for this book is available from the British Library.

ISBN 978 1 84668 332 9

Mixed Sources
Product group from well-managed
forests and other controlled sources
www.fsc.org   Cert no. TT-COC-002769
© 1996 Forest Stewardship Council

Contents

Figures

Acknowledgements

Many people have contributed a great deal to the writing of this book. I thank my good friend Duncan Baillie for his encouragement that reignited a stalled project at an opportune time, and for his flow of suggestions, questions and comments that added so much to the quality of the analysis. I thank my wife, Kathy, who not only contributed the very apt title for the book but also added greatly to its readability by objecting strenuously to obscure jargon wherever it crept in.

I also thank my very able associates at Lombard Street Research who have stimulated a continuous flow of ideas and reined in some of my over-enthusiastic forays. I especially thank Peter Allen, the managing director of Lombard Street Research, for his unflagging support that was crucial to get this book published. In addition, I would like to thank Stephen Brough and the staff at Profile Books for their invaluable help in improving its presentation.

PUT NOT THY TRUST IN FIAT MONEY

Fiat money is paper money declared by a government to be legal tender, despite the fact that it cannot be converted into gold, silver or another currency, and is not backed by reserves. Fiat money achieves value only from a government's order (or 'fiat') that it must be accepted as a means of payment. It is costless to produce, so governments have caused public distress by issuing too much fiat money throughout its history.

'Paper money eventually returns to its intrinsic value – zero.'

Voltaire

'You have to choose between trusting to the natural stability of gold and the natural stability of the honesty and intelligence of the members of the Government. And, with due respect for these gentlemen, I advise you, as long as the Capitalist system lasts, to vote for gold.'

George Bernard Shaw

'It is well enough that people of the nation do not understand our banking and monetary system, for if they did, I believe there would be a revolution before morning.'

Henry Ford

Introduction

Two hundred and thirty-three years after the publication of *An Inquiry into the Nature and Causes of the Wealth of Nations*, Adam Smith would have been intrigued by the 60-odd years of rising prosperity after the Second World War – the longest unbroken boom since the beginning of the 17th century. Now, unfortunately, the nature and causes of this extraordinary boom are shifting into reverse and the risk of an impoverishment of nations demands attention.

Any belief that globalisation combined with modern know-how and policies alone created this amazing period of rising wealth is misplaced. World trade and global mobility of capital were higher before the First World War than today because the gold standard employed capital more effectively than fiat money (money created by government decree). The Great Depression, the Second World War and the post-war reconstruction suppressed consumption for two decades, creating enormous pent-up consumer demand. In addition, an unparalleled baby boom started after the war and meeting the growing needs of all those babies as they grew up and entered the labour force meant that strong consumer demand would continue for a long time.

But demand cannot become consumption unless people can pay for what they want. Those who could repaid their debts in the Depression, and those who could not defaulted, so household and business debt was extremely low at the end of the Depression. Incomes were high during the war, but few could buy anything more than absolute necessities. Private-sector savings were very high and the financial system was very liquid at the end of the war. This enabled high levels of investment during and after the post-war reconstruction. The only restraint on growth was the availability of raw materials and labour, so a long period of prosperity was inevitable. Its very length imbued people with the idea that prosperity is the birthright of everyone.

Those who believe this will continue to be the case are destined to be disappointed because all the factors that created that remarkable period of prosperity have now reversed. Historically, each new generation was substantially larger than the preceding one but, since 1971, each new generation in the OECD has been about 60% of the size of its predecessor. Growth rates of population, labour forces and gross domestic product (GDP) are falling in many nations, while excessive borrowing, consumption and investment have created credit bubbles that have burst and threaten significant credit liquidation. In addition, unsustainable international imbalances of saving and investment must be corrected and the rising relative costs of energy, water and food will hinder efforts to promote the expected growth in living standards.

Obese governments will be an added problem

Governments are the biggest beneficiaries of inflation because a fiscal multiplier makes their revenues expand and contract more than nominal output, so they happily mandated fiat money in order to inflate as much as they wanted (as will be explained in Chapter 4). High global growth in the last quarter of a century and capital gains taxes from the serial asset booms multiplied government revenues in most developed nations. Revenues greatly exceeded forecasts; yet spending grew even faster, so governments ran up big fiscal deficits in the good years, leaving nothing for support in lean years. Falling output and asset prices have increased spending and reversed the fiscal multiplier, so fiscal deficits are soaring even higher and are now crowding out the more efficient private sector.

Two big problems stand in the way of slimming obese governments. First, most nations could greatly reduce their fiscal problems by not supporting unprofitable businesses. This would free savings for investment in profitable businesses that would increase government revenues. Subsidising business is unnecessary in many industrial nations because business saving is the biggest component of saving. Even so, government subsidises big business because it employs lots of voters and contributes generously to election campaign funds. Political parties dare not jeopardise these institutions. Second, people are now looking to governments to ease the pain of the credit bubbles bursting and the recession. Although this may be legitimate in short-term crisis management, in the longer term they are looking in the wrong direction.

The great danger is that governments will prove to have seized this golden opportunity to increase their long-term powers of meddling and influence, and, having rushed in with big fiscal and monetary stimulation packages as well as bailouts or guarantees for financial and non-financial institutions, pushing them out of this position will be a major challenge. This is unfortunate because a lot of research shows small government is better government. The journal *Public Choice* concluded from American figures from 1929 to 1986 that maximum productivity growth occurs when government expenditures total about 20% of GDP, yet all OECD governments spend far more. Government spending was 33% higher in the 15 European Union (EU) nations than in the US, yet American economic output per head was more than 40% higher. Real economic growth in the US was over 50% faster and the percentage of unemployed without a job for more than 12 months was 11.8% in the US compared with 41.9% in the EU 15.

A lot of government spending is counterproductive. For example, since New Zealand abolished all 30 agricultural subsidies in 1985, farm productivity has grown and farming's share of GDP has risen spectacularly. Similarly, in the US President Clinton signed the Welfare Reform Act in 1996. It limited receipt of welfare benefits from the federal government to a lifetime maximum of five years. The number claiming benefits shrank by 60%, the number of single mothers at work rose by 30% and the incomes of these families rose dramatically. The Index of Child and Youth Well-being has improved almost every year since 1995. In 2000, the number of children being placed for fostering fell for the first time since 1980 and has continued falling. Even cases of child malnutrition have fallen.[1]

Nevertheless, public perceptions and popularity trump results and even the most counterproductive programmes persist. Government programmes do not go through markets so no one can know their value, and government accounting systems do not reveal their true cost. Governments do not worry about such niceties as cost effectiveness and efficiency as they can always extract more money from taxpayers. Chapter 1 will show that demographics in developed nations have become a negative influence on growth and exposed the pyramid scheme aspects of welfare states. As a result, most developed nations are experiencing more immigration than their citizens want and, often, their infrastructure can cope with.

Reducing government improves the economy

Dramatic improvements in national well-being from cutting government spending in Estonia, Ireland, Latvia, New Zealand and Russia prove many, perhaps most, government programmes are counterproductive. For example, Ireland slashed government spending from 52% of GDP in 1986 to 32% in 2000 and transformed the country from 'the sick man of Europe' to the 'Celtic Tiger.' Research by Ludger Schuknecht and Vito Tanzi for the European Central Bank found that expenditure reform in the 22 industrialised countries coincided with improvement not only in fiscal and economic indicators but also in human development and institutional indicators. The percentage of working-age people in jobs rose, whereas it fell in non-reformers. Moreover, cutting spending helped the poorest people. Faster growth and targeted spending more than offset the minor effects on income distribution.[2]

Flatter tax gradients penalise saving and investment less and so raise revenue much less destructively than steeply graduated taxes. For example, the highest federal marginal tax rate in the US dropped from 91% in 1961 to 70% in 1965. Income tax revenue not only rose at a much faster rate in the years following the tax cut but also greatly exceeded expectations. The taxes paid by the highest earners exceeded expectations by the greatest amounts. The discovery that lower tax rates change people's economic behaviour, stimulate growth and create more tax revenues has led to reduced tax rates and flattened bracket gradients in many nations.

Slim governments are more likely to embrace beneficial policies, such as a stable monetary regime, which encourages economic activity. Obese governments are more likely to indulge in loose money and the resulting inflation can destroy confidence and cripple investment. Lightly regulated markets encourage efficient allocation of resources, whereas heavy regulation results in inefficiency and needlessly high costs. Similarly, free trade raises productivity and boosts living standards, but protectionism saddles nations with high costs and bottlenecks. Obese governments own and allocate resources; slim governments let tradition and law secure private property, so owners can utilise their resources efficiently.

Lowering the level of dishonesty in the ruling elite has raised living standards in many nations, for example China. Bribery, lying, favouritism and letting noisy minorities impose on the majority are obvious forms of dishonesty; secretiveness, excess regulation, inflation, arbitrariness and protectionism are more complex forms of dishonesty that disrupt markets and inhibit entrepreneurship.

Governments are running into major problems

The rich have enjoyed the lion's share of the income gains, so rises in living standards have been disappointingly small for many people. For example, US Census Bureau figures show the median real income for male, full-time, year-round workers in the US was lower in 2006 than in 1972. The gap between the rich and the poor is high and rising in both developed and emerging nations. Urban incomes are much higher than rural ones, especially in emerging nations (over triple in China) and the disparities are widening. The growing difference between expectations and reality is creating growing social tensions, and special interest groups are adding to these tensions by predicting poverty, crime, chaos or terror when proposed fiscal reforms threaten their perks.

Governments are trying to paper over these tensions by emphasising public fears of social disintegration, external aggression and economic adversity, but governments are the means by which minorities impose their will on the majority. The beneficiaries strenuously oppose every proposal to cut benefits even if, like the New Zealand farmers, they would be better off accepting the reform. Strikes and rioting are rising again as high unemployment and widening income gaps cause dissatisfaction over the way governments are handling today's problems. Competition to retain 'benefits' is forcing governments to placate the most powerful special interest groups, regardless of how badly this favouritism affects the rest of the nation.

Negative demographics and the rising costs of energy (see Chapter 1) and economic growth moving from developed to emerging nations (see Chapter 2) have slowed growth in developed nations. Lower growth is raising government spending while the fiscal multiplier is reducing revenues even more than the reduction of output growth. Fiscal stimulation and bailouts are adding to already soaring government deficits. Sovereign debt is rising rapidly and governments have begun to reduce benefits and services, for example by increasing the age at which pensions become payable and reducing the frequency of garbage collections.

Some governments will be unable to fulfil the commitments they have made. Bank guarantees have not yet been fulfilled by Iceland, are causing Ireland significant problems and have caused credit downgrades elsewhere. The fast growth of some small nations resulted from rapidly growing current account deficits and the associated import of capital. Credit Suisse estimated the total current account of eastern Europe (excluding Russia) fell from a surplus of 6% of GDP in 2004 to a deficit of 6% of GDP in 2008. The end of the credit cycle cut off the inward flow of capital to these nations. Those with slimmed down governments are readjusting rapidly; others need international agencies to bail them out.

The resurgence of big government is a major negative for world growth. This, together with the reversal in the factors underlying output growth and the end of the credit bubble, may bring more changes in the next quarter-century than were seen in the last half-century. The changes will affect all sectors of the economy and of society. This book explains how we got into the mess we are in and what is being done about it, and predicts probable outcomes.

- Chapter 1 explains basic economic concepts and describes two structural impediments to the efforts to raise living standards: demographic changes and the rising relative prices of the three basic necessities of life – energy, water and food.
- Chapter 2 examines the international context, showing that economic leadership has gravitated towards emerging nations but financial leadership has not. It also shows how political leadership is evolving and the effects of geopolitical tensions.
- Chapter 3 traces the evolution of the credit bubble and its collapse. It analyses the problems the collapse has created and the deflationary forces it has unleashed, and goes on to examine whether or not a little inflation is a good thing.

- Chapter 4 shows why the gold standard was a better monetary system than fiat money and the problems high leverage has caused. It shows that we have ignored the major source of risk in financial markets and suggests a way to eliminate irresponsible lending.
- Chapter 5 explains why the main problem is private-sector solvency, not liquidity or lack of bank lending. It shows economies are weaker than most people think, populist solutions do not work and emerging nations will not bail developed nations out of their problems.
- Chapter 6 looks at how monetary policy affects financial markets, the rise of risk aversion, the problems caused by structured finance and derivatives, the role of hedge funds and private equity, and the outlook for fixed income investments, equity markets, commodities, real estate and currencies.
- Chapter 7 discusses the long-term effects of government interference in the economy. It goes on to show that more saving is essential for growth in developed nations. It explains fundamental changes that are occurring and shows a way forward.

1

Structural impediments to rising living standards

The UN International Conference on Population and Development in Cairo, Egypt, in September 1994 revealed that global fertility rates were half of what they had been in 1972. The *2006 Revision of the Official United Nations Population Estimates and Projections* shows that global fertility rates continued to fall in the next decade. Fertility levels are below replacement level in all 45 of the more developed countries, which account for 19% of the world's population, and in 28 developing countries with 25% of the world's population. Immigration is projected to double the natural increase (births less deaths) in Belgium, Canada, Hong Kong, Luxembourg, Singapore, Spain, Sweden and Switzerland, and to offset an excess of deaths over births in Austria, Bosnia, the Channel Islands, Greece, Italy, Portugal, Slovakia and Slovenia.

Figure 1.1 shows population growth in less developed and least developed nations will be faster than in more developed nations, but a downward trend is clear in all three. It started in the early 1950s in the more developed nations, in the late 1960s in less developed nations and in the early 1990s in the least developed nations. Emigration notwithstanding, the populations of both less and least developed nations will keep growing throughout the forecast period, but at ever slower rates. Population growth is important to the economy

Figure 1.1 **Population growth by degree of development**

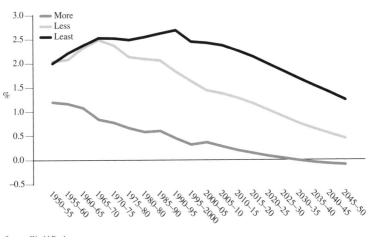

Source: World Bank

because no nation has found a way to prosper in the long term with a falling population. Japan's ageing population and falling labour force are sufficient to explain its minimal growth in the past 19 years, and Russia's falling population was a major cause of the break-up of the Soviet Union.

Ageing populations slow output growth

The average age in a nation rises as the rate of growth of the population slows, so average ages are highest in the more developed nations, lower in the less developed nations and lowest in the least developed nations. The most important effect of an ageing population is the falling growth and then decline in the working-age population, people aged 15–65. Changes in the working-age population are important for two reasons.

First, soon after joining the labour force people tend to move into separate dwellings and buy furniture, cars and so on. This bulge in personal consumption is an important component of domestic demand. Output growth tends to fall as populations age, because when fewer people enter the labour force, this slows growth in the demand for output (housing, furniture, cars, etc) far more than the changes in labour force numbers would apparently indicate. Second, output growth is the product of the increased number of workers times the increase in output per worker (labour productivity). Slower growth in the labour force reduces the rate of output growth, which in turn reduces the investment needed to expand capacity. Lower rates of net investment reduce the growth in productivity in the overall capital stock, which lowers the rate of output growth even further. Labour productivity and capital productivity together constitute multifactor (also known as 'total-factor') productivity.

The number of people of working age rises rapidly in nations with young populations and high fertility rates, such as India, so the potential growth rate in their output is high. India's working-age population should grow by over 2% a year over the next five years (see Figure 1.2). Turning its vast army of working age people who are either unemployed or surviving on subsistence agriculture into a 21st-century workforce could more than double the long-term average rise in multifactor productivity of 2% a year that industrial nations have enjoyed since the Industrial Revolution. Thus, India's long-term potential growth rate is probably $2 + 4 = 6\%$ a year.

Nations with older populations and low fertility rates, such as Japan, have declining working age populations, so the potential growth rate of their economies is low. The UN projects the number of working-age people in Japan to decline by 0.7% a year over the next five years (see Figure 1.3). It must raise its retirement age, employ a larger proportion of the people aged 15–65, promote immigration and/or raise multifactor productivity above the long-term average to raise its potential growth rate above $-0.7 + 2 = 1.3\%$ a year. Most

Figure 1.2 **Growth in population (15–64 yrs) in Brazil, Canada, China, India and Russia**

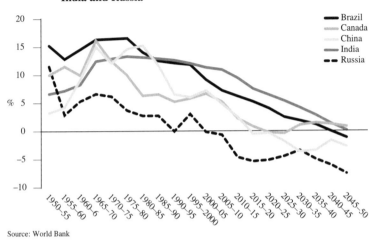

Source: World Bank

Figure 1.3 **Growth in population (15–64 yrs) in France, Germany, Japan, UK and US**

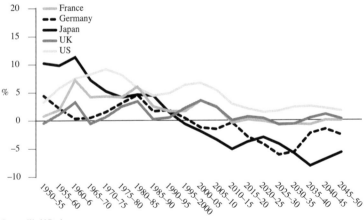

Source: World Bank

low-growth nations are adopting some or all of these methods to increase potential growth rates. For example, Japan is raising its retirement age and its labour force has remained stable (rather than declining as the forecast predicted), so its potential growth rate remained at 2% a year until the current recession.

High investment accelerates growth

Businesses must keep replacing obsolete and worn-out plant and equipment. New productive facilities are more efficient than old ones and their increased productivity reduces the investment required to maintain level of output. The replacement of productive facilities raises productivity and so expands a nation's productive capacity.[3] US GDP has grown about 2% a year and business investment has been almost exactly equal to its consumption of fixed capital. This means investment to replace facilities alone can expand productive capacity by up to 2% a year. Growth rates higher than that require additional investment to build new plant and equipment. However, construction must be completed before production can rise to fill the additional demand, so the growth rates of investment are higher than the growth rates of output when GDP is growing at more than 1–2% a year. Every 1% a year rise in output growth above that range requires investment growth of 3–4% a year in low investment economies, and more in high investment economies.

As noted above, India's potential growth rate from a rising working-age population and productivity is 6+% a year. With its emphasis on services, India is a low investment economy; investment would have to grow by $(6 - 2) \times 3 = 12\%$ to $(6 - 1) \times 4 = 20\%$ a year to maintain 6+% a year growth in GDP. This much higher rate of growth in investment raises India's potential growth to about 8% a year, a level it finally attained in the 21st century.

This virtuous circle of rising investment creating rising

consumption, which then requires more investment and so on, is called the investment accelerator. However, investment requires an equal amount of saving, so investment can grow only as fast as saving. The main factor limiting the rate of output growth that the investment accelerator can produce in nations with ample supplies of working-age people is lack of saving. Chapter 2 will show how nations can augment low domestic saving by importing foreign saving.

The investment accelerator can maintain high potential growth rates in most emerging nations, but they are facing a catch-22 situation. They must stimulate domestic demand to achieve their potential, but must also turn their inadequate and disjointed social support plans into modern social security safety nets to lower savings rates and so increase the propensity to consume. Few emerging nations are succeeding in this transition, so low growth in industrial nations should more than offset the higher growth in emerging nations and average world growth should fall.

Avoiding the investment decelerator

America is the only developed nation in which the working-age population may grow fast enough for the investment accelerator to keep boosting potential growth indefinitely. The older populations in the other more developed nations will keep their potential GDP growth below that of the less developed nations for decades. Working-age population growth will be low to negative in the UK and France and negative throughout the period in Germany and Japan, dropping their potential growth rates to 2% a year or less. Replacing obsolete and worn-out plant and equipment can raise capacity by about 2% a year, so lack of net investment can turn the investment accelerator into a decelerator and reduce their growth rates to zero or less.

In Japan, for example, the government is already overstretched and so cannot spend more to augment GDP. Japan's population is both falling and ageing, so consumption is unlikely to grow at the rate of 3% or so required to sustain GDP growth at 2%. Japan must therefore export more than it imports to offset the lack of domestic demand. Failing to do so would reverse the investment accelerator. Every 1% drop in output below 1% growth would reduce investment by 3–4%, accelerating the decline in output growth.

Low-growth nations need trade surpluses to achieve their potential growth rates and so must export saving (see Chapter 2). Japan faces decades of deflation because a cultural reluctance to export saving keeps domestic returns on saving low. The lack of income from savings is hurting domestic consumption. Many nations, such as Germany and much of eastern Europe, are in a similar position and many more will join them in the coming years. The investment decelerator has been shrinking output in many nations in Africa, and their experiences show how hard it is to overcome this disadvantage. The sharp reversals in growth when Japan raised consumption taxes and when it tightened monetary policy show mistaken policies will impede output growth much more in the low-growth future than in the high-growth past.

China and Russia face the investment decelerator too. China is a high-growth nation that may quickly turn into a low-growth nation because its one-child policy is reducing the growth rate of its working-age population quickly. The working-age population will begin to fall by about 2015, which should begin reducing China's potential output growth by 2020. The commodities boom gave Russia great prosperity but, with a falling population and an average decline of about 1% a year in its working-age population after 2010, it is unlikely to regain the superpower status it is avidly seeking. Russia will be hard pressed to grow at all when the commodity boom ends. However, China and Russia will have less trouble avoiding the investment decelerator as they are not welfare states.

Welfare states are essentially giant pyramid schemes because they rely on an ever increasing inflow of workers to pay for the benefits given to the rising number of non-workers. Welfare states prospered when labour forces and productivity grew fast enough to keep the cost of providing the benefits at tolerably low levels per worker. However, the fall in the birth rate in more developed nations that began in the 1950s has slowed, and will continue to slow, growth in their working-age populations. The burden of providing benefits has grown intolerably high in some nations and they are cutting benefit levels. Immigration can partly offset the slowdown in the growth of the working-age population, but it is a temporary palliative at best.

Pension problems will reduce growth even more

Pensions transfer wealth from working-age people to senior citizens. Defined-benefit pension plans pay specified ratios of earnings; defined-contribution plans amass a sum that is used to buy pensions at the market rate at time of retirement. The rising cost of defined-benefit plans has raised mandatory contributions so high that ever more people try to avoid contributing. Governments are trying to keep the required contributions down by raising retirement ages and/or curtailing pension benefits. Businesses are trying to avoid the rising costs of defined-benefit plans by converting to defined-contribution plans, thereby transferring the risk to their employees. Unionised workers are strenuously resisting any change to pension plans.

People of working age create all the output in the economy, but have no prospect of consuming the pensioners' share, regardless of whether or not pension plans are funded. This burden of supplying pensioners' consumption was light and widely spread half a century ago when labour forces grew rapidly and there were many workers per pensioner. Contribution rates had to be raised as populations aged and the ratio of workers to retired people fell. The generosity of pension benefits determines the number of workers per pensioner

Figure 1.4 **People of working age per pensioner in Brazil, Canada, China, India and Russia**

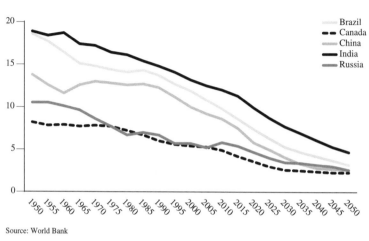

Source: World Bank

at which the pension burden becomes intolerable. The number of working-age people per pensioner has fallen below four in both Japan and Germany. Pensions have become an intolerable burden in Japan but not in Germany, because Japan's pensions are more generous than Germany's.

Figure 1.4 shows that the number of persons of working age per person of pension age in the BRIC countries and Canada will fall over the forecast period. Brazil and India give small means-tested pensions from pay-as-you-go plans. China's ageing population is raising the cost of its pensions at an alarming rate, and pensions there are badly underfunded. All three nations need serious pension reform that will raise the cost of pensions dramatically. Russia put its pension system on a relatively sound footing in 2003 by moving to a funded plan with required contributions of 20% of wages. Canada has a fully funded pension plan and is unlikely to have to reduce benefits or raise retirement ages before the 2020s, and maybe not even then.

Figure 1.5 **People of working age per pensioner in France, Germany, Japan, UK and US**

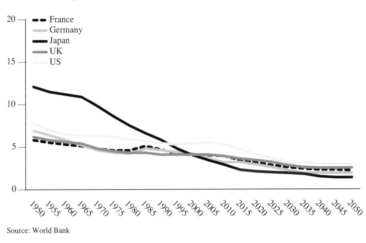

Source: World Bank

Figure 1.5 shows the number of persons of working age per person of pension age in the five largest industrial nations. They all will be forced into raising the retirement age and/or curtailing pension benefits sometime in the forecast period. Even senior citizens in the US will ultimately lose their long battle to retain their 'entitlement' to overly generous retirement income and health benefits.

Japan has the biggest pension problem among the developed nations. Its pension benefits have been overly generous because of the high number of workers per pensioner until the 1990s. Now, however, Japan has the oldest population and the lowest number of workers per pensioner. It has become a world leader in the science of robotics in an effort to create synthetic workers. Even so, pension contribution rates have risen so high that workers are searching for loopholes. Rising pension costs contributed so much to Japan's out-sized government deficits that a 2004 pension reform law raised annual mandatory contributions year from 13.6% of income in 2004

18

to 18.3% in 2017 and slashed benefits from 59.3% to 50.2% of final income. However, pension experts say the 2004 reforms are far from the final answer to Japan's problems.

The number of workers available to support each pensioner will fall in all ten of the nations we have looked at and pension problems will grow until either birth rates begin rising or robots develop into synthetic people. Cuts in Japanese pension benefits and low returns on saving are hurting current consumption and making it harder for Japan to attain its potential growth rate.

The current renewable energy programme is a huge waste

The second big impediment to rising living standards is rising energy costs. Generating electricity consumes about 40% of the fuel we produce, heating our homes and businesses consumes about 30% and transportation consumes the other 30%. The accidents at Three Mile Island and Chernobyl together with desires to reduce both dependence on unreliable sources of energy and CO_2 emissions inspired frenzied activity to develop renewable sources of electricity. The sources politicians chose are technically, economically and socially unsound, so they have added little to world generating capacity and yet increased the cost of energy significantly. There is little evidence of any change in the foreseeable future.

For example, the political favourite, wind power, costs four times as much as conventionally produced power. It operates only one-sixth to one-third of the time and so requires full back-up from conventional sources. Worse, the extreme variability of wind generated power is wreaking havoc on the grid systems in Denmark and Germany, the nations with the highest proportion of wind power. Worst of all, a 2004 report for the German federal economics ministry showed the lifetime reduction in carbon emissions from wind power is zero, largely because of the awesome amount of steel that is used.

Persisting with the development of such expensive power is escalating the migration of economic leadership to emerging nations and so costing developing nations millions of jobs (see Chapter 2). In addition, emphasising exotic sources of power has sidetracked effective existing technologies such as co-generation. Britain wastes enough heat in producing electricity to heat the entire nation. Many other nations are in a similar position, so co-generation could slash carbon emissions. The EU says it wants to raise co-generation from 10% of electricity production in 2001 to 18% in 2010, but the efforts are minuscule and the target will not be met. Unlike solar panels and windmills, co-generation is neither obvious nor expensive and so generates neither a following nor a lobby to promote it.

Coal, uranium and natural gas have added greatly to world generating capacity at far less cost than renewable sources and can satisfy our rising electricity needs far into the future. Gas is the cheapest and coal suffers from a bad press. However, 'clean coal' generating plants can now be as ecologically benign as gas-fired plants.

Electricity from clean coal generally costs about a quarter more than electricity from gas, but a new power plant design, Thermo-energy Integrated Power System, may soon change that. This system combusts carbonaceous fuels, including coal, oil, natural gas, municipal waste and biomass, under pressure in a furnace surrounded by pipes filled with water that turns to steam and spins turbines to produce electricity. Only ash, used in making concrete, is left in the furnace. The pollutants (sulphur oxides, nitrogen oxides, mercury and particulate matter) are extracted from the hot exhaust fumes, separated and packaged for commercial use. Some of the carbon dioxide goes back to the furnace to exploit the residual energy in it and the rest can be turned into a compressed liquid, ready for underground storage. All this can be done in power plants one-tenth the size of conventional plants which would fit comfortably close to consumers in large cities. Initial tests show it should be a cheap source of electricity. A Thermoenergy Integrated Power System demonstration plant can produce zero-pollution, carbon-captured electricity for 8 cents a kilowatt-hour (kWh) compared to the 2006 average American retail cost of 9.8 cents.[4]

At present interest rates, nuclear power costs about twice as much as power from gas-fired plants. Much of the excess cost is a result of unwarranted fears of both radiation and reprocessing spent fuel into nuclear weapons, artificially raising waste disposal and decommissioning costs. The danger of radiation has been greatly exaggerated. Japan, the nation worst affected by radiation by far, has an older and arguably healthier population with a longer life expectancy than any other major nation. No radiation at all escaped in the Three Mile Island accident, and radiation from the explosion that destroyed Reactor #4 at Chernobyl in 1986 has caused 56 deaths to date, not the 9,000 that were forecast, all of them among the workers who were sent in to clean up the mess with no protective clothing.[5]

Moreover, those nuclear reactors embodied the worst design characteristics. Heavy-water and gas-cooled generators greatly lower the risk of such accidents – the former because the high pressure is distributed over many tubes rather than a single core vessel and the latter because of the much slower temperature rise in the event of a loss of coolant. Heavy-water generators also avoid the need to enrich fuel and so do not produce weapons-grade fissionable material.

Thorium-fuelled nuclear generators both greatly reduce radioactive waste and do not produce weapons-grade fissionable material. Thorium is more abundant than uranium and all of it is suitable for fuel. However, processing thorium is expensive and the uranium lobby has succeeded in derailing interest in it as a potential energy source. As a result, some of the problems of processing thorium have not yet been solved – and we do not need to solve them.

There is a better option than all the ideas discussed so far. The inside of the Earth is hot enough to melt rock. Enough heat to power generating plants radiates up to within 6 kilometres of the Earth's surface. About 70 countries now produce geothermal electricity totalling about 100 gigawatts. China and Hungary have the biggest readily available resources, but the US and the Philippines now produce the most geothermal electricity. In the hottest areas, steam to run the turbines may come directly from the earth as in The Geysers complex in California. Currently, electric power produced this way costs 4–6 cents per kWh. In less hot areas the hot water is used to vaporise a secondary fluid to drive the generators and the power costs 5–8 cents per kWh.

Geothermal plants could produce as much safe, clean, cheap and continuously available electricity as we could ever want. Geothermal plants have a reliability record of 90%, about the same as nuclear plants. Wind and solar power have reliability records of 25–40% and 22–35% respectively. Geothermal energy is not depleted like an oil or gas well, so qualifies for the benefits given to develop renewable energy. Any water injected is reused and the carbon footprint is about 5% of a fossil fuel plant, so geothermal is an environmentally friendly source of power.

Politics in most developed nations have skewed the biggest efforts into the most costly and least effective methods of generating electricity: wind and solar. This means their power costs will keep rising far into the future, but other nations are far more realistic. Oil is too expensive to use to generate electricity. In the Middle East in July 2008, for example, generating 1 megawatt-hour cost $17.49 from coal, $41.34 from natural gas and $79.50 from oil. As a result, Middle East oil-producing nations are building coal-fired power plants.[6] China is adding another coal-fired plant every week.

Little oil is used in generating electricity and soon little will be used for heating. Gas now supplies well over half of our heating. The cost of natural gas is extremely volatile, but it generally costs less than half as much as oil per BTU (British thermal unit) and its easy transportability means its share of the heating market will keep rising. However, the Middle East and the former Soviet Union together hold almost three-quarters of the world's natural gas reserves. They can and will interrupt supplies whenever and wherever they want. Geothermal and cogenerated electricity would lower the cost of electrical heating and also reduce dependence on unstable gas supplies, but there is no such easy alternative to oil for transportation and industrial uses, such as making plastic products.

Corn-based ethanol is the biggest waste of all

Transportation consumes about half the oil produced, industry about one-third and heating and electrical generation together the other one-sixth. That sixth will diminish through time and we can do little about the third used in industry. However, we can do plenty about the half that powers most of our transportation. Railways are electrifying, and memories of the mountains of wasted food surpluses in the past have encouraged big biofuel programmes.

Ethanol made from cane sugar waste has been powering a growing share of vehicles in Brazil for three decades. The energy output is about five times the energy input because no fossil fuels are used in processing. The ethanol costs less per unit of energy than the petrol it replaces at oil prices above $30 per barrel. Sugar-based ethanol is a viable alternative to oil, but ethanol cannot be transported in the pipelines used to transport oil and gas, raising its cost and limiting its distribution.

Grain-based ethanol is a different story. It uses more energy to make than it produces, its cost per unit of energy is many times higher than the gasoline it replaces and it deprives the world of food. The OECD estimates biofuels accounted for 60% of the growth of global consumption of cereals and vegetable oils from 2005 to 2007. This explosion of non-food demand in the context of falling supplies contributed to the soaring food prices in 2007–08. Persistence with this policy could have dire effects. The whole US corn crop could produce only enough ethanol to satisfy 15% of US automotive needs.

An estimated 100 million tonnes of grain, enough to feed 450 million people for a year, was turned into fuel in 2008 – even though food-based biofuels are highly subsidised political footballs unable to displace enough oil to make a difference. Agricultural waste, such as straw and sawdust, can make biofuels, but they too take more energy to convert than the product yields. Also, the supply of such biofuels would be limited, especially in the EU, which has banned using straw to make them. But biofuels are merely a sideshow.

The world will not run out of oil

Non-oil powered vehicles may offer a long-term reduction of depen-dency on oil but, in the short term, they all suffer from the drawbacks of excessive cost, unreliability and limited range before refuelling. Lithium ion batteries hold some promise for increasing the range of electric cars, but they are expensive and lose about 20% of their capacity each year after manufacture. Hydrogen-powered vehicles using either conventional internal combustion engines or fuel cells seem to be the best hope. General Motors wants to mass-produce hydrogen-powered cars complete with adequate refuelling stations by 2012, but the company is currently bankrupt and this three-year target is unrealistic.

Gasoline's power output per unit of mass is 3.4 times that of liquid hydrogen. The excessive volume of hydrogen complicates delivery to refuelling stations and tanks suitable for mass-produced cars have not yet been designed. On a more positive note, fuel cell technology is advancing and platinum-free electrocatalysts have been designed. Some commercial vehicles are now using fuel cells, but mass-production of hydrogen-powered cars is unlikely before 2020.

Estimates of the timing of peak oil production vary from now to not in the foreseeable future. The latter is probably more accurate. NO.

High oil prices encouraged the uncovering of big new reserves and destroyed demand. Platforms capable of drilling 5 miles down have found potentially huge oil reserves in the Gulf of Mexico and off the coast of Brazil. Other promising areas for deep drilling include the North Sea, the Nile River Delta and off the coast of West Africa. Deep-ocean drilling is relatively expensive, but far less expensive than unconventional energy sources.

Tar sands and oil from coal are economic sources of oil at prices far below the peak reached in 2008. Current production costs in the tar sands in Northern Alberta range up to about $60 a barrel. The cost of oil from coal is presently estimated at about $50 a barrel in America – and newer technologies promise to be cheaper. The products burn cleaner than those obtained from crude oil and the US has an estimated 267 billion tonnes reserve of coal, enough to produce 20 times the amount of oil in its crude oil reserves. America's first coal-to-oil plant was planned to come on line in Wyoming in 2009. Montana has vast unexploited coal fields, but no coal-to-oil plants are contemplated because converting coal to oil consumes twice as much coal and produces twice the CO_2 emissions as burning coal in a conventional power plant.

Other nations are more enthusiastic about oil from coal. Shenhua, China's biggest coal producer, has 30 coal-to-oil projects in the feasibility study or later stages. A plant using the direct conversion of coal to oil began operating in 2008 at an estimated cost of $30 a barrel and a $6 billion project with Royal Dutch Shell will come on stream in 2012. Shenhua aims to produce 30 million tonnes of oil from coal, about one-seventh of China's annual oil usage, in eight plants by 2020.

Shale oil rock has been used as a fuel for centuries. The reserves in Colorado, Utah and Wyoming contain an estimated 1.5 trillion barrels of oil, five times Saudi Arabian reserves. The total cost of synthetic crude oil from shale oil rock is estimated to be $70–90 a barrel initially, but should fall significantly as production ramps up – perhaps to less than $50 a barrel. No major shale oil project is being planned currently because 1 tonne of shale oil yields only 150 litres of oil whereas 1 tonne of coal yields 650 litres.

The amount of oil recoverable from global reserves of tar sands, coal and shale oil is many times the reserves of conventional oil – big enough to satisfy our demands for oil for decades, if not centuries. Even so, they are no panacea as they require huge initial investments, the energy return on the energy invested is only 5–10% that of conventional drilling, and they use far more water and emit more CO_2 and other pollutants.

Rising energy costs are impeding the rise in living standards

The rising use of energy and falling energy prices account for most of the huge rise in living standards since the Industrial Revolution began. That golden era ended in 1973 with the shock of the 13-fold rise in the price of oil from 1973 to 1980 (see Figure 1.6). Higher energy costs were a big factor in the average rate of GDP growth falling by about one-quarter after 1980. Other energy prices also rose and the recessions following the spikes in oil prices in 1973–74, 1979–80, 1990, 2000 and 2007–08 show the cost of energy is a crucial factor in economic cycles.

The higher energy prices reduced demand. Energy consumption in the US halved from about 18,000 BTU per dollar of real GDP in 1971 to about 9,000 BTU in 2005, according to the Skeptical Optimist,[7] an average rate of decline of 2% a year. The rise in real oil prices from 1999 to 2008 was similar to the 1973–80 spike over about the same time span. Real energy prices should continue the upward trend since 1973, so energy consumption per unit of GDP should halve over the next three decades or so.

Even though the world will never run out of oil, fear of imminent peak production raised prices fast enough to turn oil into an

Figure 1.6 **Oil prices in US$, 1861–2009**

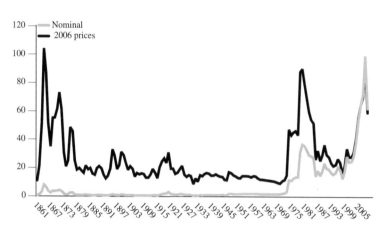

Source: Energy Information Administration

'investment'. In addition, political instability constrained supply while adding to strategic reserves increased demand. Investors bought one year's production of oil in 2005–07, greatly increasing apparent demand. Many people believe this did not affect the spot price of oil because investors bought contracts for future delivery and rolled them forward instead of taking delivery. This belief is mistaken.

The market for oil is finely balanced. OPEC is the swing producer and tries to keep inventories near normal by increasing (decreasing) supply when spot prices rise (fall) relative to futures prices. This constant matching of current supply and demand removed the spot market from the oil pricing mechanism. The futures market took over and investors bid oil prices to levels that slashed demand. Falling demand and the credit crunch panicked investors and their selling drove oil prices far below the marginal cost of production, about $50 a barrel.

The greater reversal in investment demand in the current cycle slashed real prices faster than in the 1973–80 cycle, but considerably less in percentage terms because the cost of finding and producing oil has risen sharply. The real price will rise far into the future, but by how much?

Credit Suisse analysed the probable prices of oil with global growth of 3–4% a year, about 0.5% a year on either side of trend growth.[8] They used the calculated price elasticity from 1980 to 2008 (higher) and from 1983 to 2008 (lower). Assuming no increase in the supply of oil from 2008, they calculated the price of oil would range from an annual average price in 2008 dollars of $77–164 a barrel using the lower price elasticity and $54–101 using the higher price elasticity. A real price of $101 in ten years would entail an average rise of about 7% a year, enough to preclude any rise in living standards in developed nations.

Cold fusion is the only hope of avoiding rising energy prices. It is a controversial subject because there is no satisfactory theoretical explanation for the amount of heat that cold fusion experiments have produced. The experiments have been replicated many times, but many replication efforts have failed. Is the experimental error in the reported successes or the failures? No one can say with certainty, but two decades after the original experiment, it is safe to rule out commercial use of cold fusion for decades. Even so, lack of water is a greater threat to rising living standards than expensive energy.

We are using unsustainable amounts of water

The world's population has doubled since 1950, but global demand for water is doubling every 21 years. Only 2.5% of the world's water is fit for human consumption and two-thirds of that is locked away in icecaps and glaciers. Unlike other commodities, no new water reserves will suddenly be discovered, there is no substitute for water and just about everything and everyone relies on it. As a result, the International Water Management Institute estimates that one-third of the world's population is short of water. Worse, we have already reached a point that, according to previous reports, we should not reach until 2025, so the situation is deteriorating fast.

Big reserves of fresh, potable water lie in underground aquifers that provide more than half of the water in America, up to 80% in Europe and Russia and 25% worldwide. They contain 30 times more water than all the world's lakes and hundreds of times more than all the world's reservoirs. Precipitation recharges shallow aquifers naturally and they can be recharged artificially, but the vast deep aquifers took millions of years to form and replenish themselves extremely slowly. Water in deep aquifers is being depleted and is as irreplaceable as the water of glaciers. Water levels in some deep aquifers, such as the giant Ogallala aquifer that irrigates about one-third of the US corn crop, are dropping at alarming rates and wells have already run dry in some areas.

Depletion of global groundwater supplies exceeds replenishment by an estimated 4% annually, so water tables are falling in nations containing over half the world's people. For example, water tables in Phoenix have dropped 400 feet in the last 50 years. Overconsumption of water is drying up lakes and rivers on every continent. The Aral Sea has shrunk by 75% since 1967 and Lake Chad by 95% since 1963. China's Qinghai province has lost about 2,000 of its 4,077 lakes and Hebei province around Beijing has lost 969 of its 1,052 lakes. The Dead Sea is 82 feet lower than it was 50 years ago. One in ten of the world's major rivers fail to reach the sea for part of the year, including the Colorado, Yellow, Indus and Ganges. The Colorado delivered 17.5 million acre feet to six south-western states in 1922, but delivers only 11.5 million acre feet today.

Agriculture uses 70% of the world's water, business uses 22% and households use 8%. About half the water allocated to agriculture and 30–40% of the rest disappears in pipe and canal leakages and illegal tapping. Furthermore, agricultural run-off and waste disposal pollute much of our river and lake water.

China, with 7% of the world's water and 22% of its population, faces a severe water shortage, especially in the north. Skyrocketing demand, overuse, inefficiencies, pollution and unequal distribution have produced a situation in which two-thirds of China's approximately 660 cities have less water than they need and 110 of them suffer severe shortages. Ma Jun, a leading Chinese water expert, says several cities near Beijing and Tianjin in the north-eastern region of the country could run out of water in 5–7 years. Shanghai will have to use desalinised water in the next 10 years, and then build the infrastructure to import water from south-west China. Glacial melt produces all the water in south-west China and it will not be there in anything like the capacity that will be required in about 25 years' time.[9]

Chinese industries use 10–20% more water than their counterparts in developed nations, and China's plundering of its groundwater reserves has created huge underground tunnels. Some of its wealthiest cities are sinking – by more than 6 feet during the past decade and a half in the case of Shanghai and Tianjin. Subsidence has destroyed factories, buildings and underground pipelines in Beijing and is threatening the city's main international airport.

Pollution costs China 8–12% of GDP.[10] Polluted surface water, hazardous waste, pesticides and fertilisers have polluted the aquifers in 90% of Chinese cities, according to a report by the government-run Xinhua News Agency. China has plenty of laws and regulations designed to ensure that water is clean, but factory owners and local officials do not enforce them. A 2005 survey of 509 cities revealed that only 23% of factories properly treated sewage before disposing of it. Another report showed one-third of all industrial wastewater in China and two-thirds of household sewage is released untreated. The Yangtze River receives 40% of the country's sewage and 80% of it is untreated.

Lack of water is affecting Chinese grain production, which fell from 392 million tonnes in 1998 to 358 million tonnes in 2005. That 34 million tonne shortfall is enough to feed more than 100 million Chinese. In spring 2007, the Chinese government released its first national assessment report on climate change, predicting a 30% drop in precipitation in the Huai, Liao and Hai river regions and a 37% decline in the country's wheat, rice and corn yields in the second half of the century. China has the worst problems of any major power, but it is not alone. Many nations have turned to desalinating sea water to solve their water problems.

Desalination is no panacea

Currently, between 10 and 13 billion gallons of water are desalinated per day in more than 15,000 plants. That is only about 0.2% of global water consumption, but the proportion is rising. Technological improvements have reduced the cost of desalination (excluding transportation) to $3 or $4 per 1,000 gallons, double or triple the cost of conventional water supplies.

Large amounts of energy are needed to generate the high pressure that forces the water through the membrane that filters most of the salt out of the water, so energy accounts for almost half the cost of desalination. Rising energy costs guarantee the cost of desalination will rise and supply shocks could raise it significantly. Even so, lack of water for business and residential use will not be a serious problem in most coastal areas, but transportation costs will limit how far inland it can be used.

Desalinated water is inferior to fresh water from aquifers and reservoirs as it tastes brackish and is corrosive. Boilers and hot-water tanks using desalinated water last about five years. Investment to enhance supplies of fresh water and to conserve fresh water by collecting grey water for irrigation, flushing toilets and so on will yield much greater benefits at less cost than investment in battling global warming – especially in poorer emerging nations, many of which still have rapidly growing populations and histories of polluting surface water.

The price of water is creating growing social and economic problems in many water-short nations. The rich and powerful have access to all the water they want and they often leave little for the poor, creating growing humanitarian problems. Agriculture, industrialisation and urbanisation are draining aquifers and drying up rivers and lakes at an alarming rate. Present agricultural prices are squeezing farmers out of the competition for increasingly scarce water resources and the loss of water for irrigation has created a deficit in world food production. This deficit has started a long-lasting rise in real food prices.

The price of water is lower than the cost of delivering it and will rise significantly. A Peopleandplanet.net study[11] showed the average price of water rose 27% in the US, 32% in the UK, 45% in Australia, 50% in South Africa and 58% in Canada in the five years to 2007. Even so, most of the water used, especially by agriculture, is still subsidised. Agriculture has been losing water to industry and the cities, both of which can afford to pay much more than farmers. One tonne of grain needs 1,000 tonnes of water and 1 tonne of beef needs 9,000 tonnes of water, so lack of water means lack of food.

Food shortages will become endemic

Importing tonnes of food is equivalent to importing thousands of tonnes of water, so most water-short nations are rapidly increasing their food imports. Algeria, Egypt and Mexico already import most of the grain they consume and Iran and Pakistan are catching up fast. Irrigation was a big part of the 'green revolution' that tripled world grain production between 1950 and 2000. However, the big increase in irrigation has led to an unsustainable draw on fossil water and lack of water for irrigation has begun to limit food production.

World grain production has failed to keep up with consumption in recent years – even with unsustainable water usage. China depends on irrigated land for four-fifths of its grain harvest, so is worst affected by lack of water (see above). India depends on irrigated land for three-fifths of its grain harvest, but an ever increasing number of farmers are being forced into dry land farming. Indian food grain production is stagnating and will fall in the foreseeable future.

Rice stocks at the end of the 2008 crop year were equal to 67 days of consumption, a 25-year low, and protectionism in food has begun. Most rice-producing nations have abolished import duties and either limited or banned exports of rice to preserve and build up their own stocks. Other grain stocks carried over to the next crop year have been falling for several years and are at the lowest levels relative to consumption for decades. Wheat and corn stocks at the end of the 2008 crop year were 70 days and 60 days of consumption respectively.

The UN forecasts the world's population will grow by almost half in the next 40 years. Also, rising living standards are raising meat consumption faster than population growth, and meat production consumes far more water than grain production. Lack of water is impeding the green revolution (that is, the big increase in agricultural productivity from about 1950 to about 2000), especially in China and India, which are turning from significant exporters of food to importers.[12] Shortages are uncommon as yet, but dwindling stocks of major traded grains left at the end of the crop year caused big price rises from spring/summer 2007 to April 2008. Prices of the big three – wheat, corn and rice – doubled and most other grain prices came close to doubling in that time period.

Turning food into biofuels is being blamed for the rising prices, but fear of shortages and speculation may have had a greater impact. The credit crunch has curbed speculation and bumper crops are expected in the 2009 crop year, so prices have eased back. However, rising prices for water and its increasing scarcity mean that real food prices have reached their lows and the future trend will be upwards. Rising prices for food and water should encourage conservation and, hopefully, end the waste of food in making biofuels.

World food production grew faster than world population until this century. This allowed people to eat better, and the falling price of food enhanced the rise in living standards. World population is forecast to grow by almost 50% by 2050 and emerging nations will want to eat better, so food production will have to grow by a lot more than 50% to satisfy everyone. However, using increasing amounts of irreplaceable fossil water failed to raise food production enough to meet consumption in this century and food stocks fell to levels that caused food riots and changed subsidies on food exports into bans.

The era of abundant food is over. Weather in major crop-growing regions, excluding Australia recently, has been benign for the past decade and a half, but it will not remain benign forever. One year of bad weather in a big food production area would create scarcity and a lot of arable land is being lost to desertification and urbanisation. Not only will real food prices rise, but also the ability of technology to overcome the growing reliance on diminishing supplies of fossil water is dubious. As a result, the global population could outgrow the planet's capacity to feed it. Only another green revolution equal to the last one can raise food production to the amount being con-sumed today and then keep raising production enough to meet future demands regardless of the weather.

Sea-water greenhouses are starting to offset loss to desertifica-tion, rising water prices will encourage conservation, and genetically modified grains will raise yields per acre and nutrition per unit of water. Rising food prices will end the use of food to power cars and lower meat consumption, but all that is too little too late to meet both the population growth and rising living standards in emerging nations. Rising real food prices will add to rising real energy prices to hinder rising living standards in both developed and emerging nations.

Conclusion

Demographics greatly alter the world economy over time, but they change slowly, so most forecasts ignore them. Demographic changes have slowed growth to levels that threaten to turn the investment accelerator that has generally enhanced growth in developed nations since the Second World War into a decelerator. However, many emerging nations will continue to enjoy the benefits of the invest-ment accelerator for a while yet. This is a major factor in the shift of leadership from developed nations to emerging nations that will be discussed in the next chapter.

Politics and fear of global warming have created energy policies in developed nations that defy logic, so the cost of energy is rising far faster than necessary. At the same time, emerging nations are pro-ducing vast amounts of energy at a small fraction of the cost of addi-tional energy in developed nations. Emerging national competition in both energy and labour costs guarantees output growth, and the rise in living standards in developed nations will be minimal at best.

Talk of peak oil production is rampant, but what about peak water production? Water tables are falling and lakes, rivers and wells are drying at rates that indicate we are uncomfortably close to peak water production. We will know where that peak is only after production starts to fall and it is too late to take corrective actions. Adequate water is a non-substitutable requirement of food production, and the long-held assumption that adequate water will always be available is wrong. Increasing water problems indicate that the proportion of the global population going to bed hungry at night is more likely to rise than to fall.

Population growth and rising living standards in emerging nations will keep continuous pressure on food supplies and prices, so the use of fossil water will keep increasing. The rapid retreat of glaciers means that we cannot even be certain the world can grow enough food to meet the expectations of the current population in perpetuity, let alone the forecast population. The availability and price of water and food will soon displace the availability and price of energy as the world's greatest economic concern.

2

Emerging nations are becoming global leaders

Industrial nations are trying to stimulate consumption to boost output growth, but that is the same as a poor man trying to consume more in order to become rich. A poor man does not become rich by consuming more, but by consuming less and investing the amount saved. The same is true for nations. Chapter 1 showed how saving and investment boosts growth with the investment accelerator, but that is only part of the benefit of high rates of growth in investment.

New plants and equipment are more productive than old. High rates of growth in investment lower the average age of productive facilities, making them more efficient and raising national productivity. Productivity determines a nation's standard of living so, other things being equal, the higher the rate of growth in investment, the faster living standards rise. Investment requires an equal amount of saving, so output and living standards usually rise faster in nations with high rates of saving than in those with low rates of saving. However, nations with low rates of domestic saving can raise their rates of growth in investment by importing savings.

Current account surpluses automatically export equal amounts of domestic saving and current account deficits automatically import equal amounts of foreign saving. Thus nations can run current account deficits to import the foreign saving needed to fund the investment that exceeds their domestic savings. Many analysts believe that chronic current account deficits signify bad policies, and so must create problems. However, Canada prospered for many years with big current account deficits because foreigners wanted to invest enough in Canada to offset its current account deficits – and often even more.

Any nation can keep running big current account deficits as long as foreigners want to invest amounts in that nation that at least equal its current account deficits.

Ample supplies of well-educated, low-cost labour and growth-oriented policies in some emerging nations are attracting investment from more developed nations in a broad range of businesses. Investment in new facilities in less developed nations, some of which employ highly skilled workers, has created global markets in labour, capital, most goods and some services. This globalisation has greatly increased competition, forcing businesses in industrial nations to cut costs wherever possible, and encouraged the movement of production to low labour cost locations.

Inferior physical and legal infrastructures, lack of training and political problems make workers less productive in emerging nations than in industrial nations. However, wage differences often more than offset those disadvantages, so companies in industrial nations are locating much of their new investment in manufacturing, warehousing and tradable services in emerging nations. This is raising the growth rates of investment and output in emerging nations, especially those with low rates of saving.

Emerging market workers limit income gains

Investment, productivity and living standards are rising much faster in the less developed nations with policies encouraging domestic saving and inward investment than in industrial nations. Microsoft claims Asia is now the world centre for growth and innovation. Market analysts have predicted the Asia-Pacific region will expand twice as fast as North America. The internet has enabled trained workers in less developed nations with various qualifications to attract employment from more developed nations ever higher up the income scale.

Thus, for the first time, competition from emerging nations is limiting wage and employment gains for white-collar as well as blue-collar workers in industrial nations. As a result, economic leadership is gravitating towards emerging nations – with far-reaching consequences. China is now the third largest economy in the world measured in dollars at market prices and the second largest measured in purchasing power parity. America now consumes so much Chinese production, causing huge US trade deficits with China, that some people claim America's manufacturing industry is located in China.

India is the 12th largest economy at market prices and the fourth largest in purchasing power parity. Emerging nation demand for commodities and energy, especially Chinese and Indian, affects world markets far more than industrial nation demand. Labour in emerging nations has benefited greatly from globalisation, as both employment growth and wage levels have soared. Even so, globalisation has quadrupled the potential number of available workers, and the competition from these lower-paid workers is exerting downward pressure on wage rates in industrial nations.

Moreover, millions more potential workers in the least developed nations could enter the global workforce if their nations replicate what the emerging nations have already done – that is, rise up the corruption perception index prepared by Transparency International. (Workers from least developed nations joining the global labour force would be bad news for workers in both emerging and developed nations.) The corruption perception index ranks the degree of corruption seen by people doing business in that country, with the least corrupt nation at the top. The correlation between a nation's rank on the index and its rank on the income scale is high. Developed nations dominate the top quintile and big emerging nations, such as Brazil, China and India, have risen to the second quintile.

In the 2008 index, Russia is the only economically important nation ranked below the second quintile. Most of the lowest places are occupied by least developed nations. They are least developed because they are run by kleptocracies that skim a share off everything and pocket most, if not all, government-to-government aid. The highest concentration of such nations is in Africa where 42% of people paid bribes to receive the services they needed, twice the percentage of the next highest area, Asia Pacific, and 20 times that of the lowest area, North America. Much of the massive aid to Africa has done nothing more than support tin-pot dictators – and so has been wasted at best and counterproductive at worst.

International competition for jobs caused slow employment growth for several years during the recovery in industrial nations in the 1990s. Even greater competition caused even slower employment growth in the 2002–07 recovery and wage rates, particularly for unskilled and semi-skilled workers, have not kept pace with inflation in many nations. Living standards for lower-paid workers in industrial nations are not rising, even though their labour forces are growing slowly, if at all, because their output is barely enough to justify current employment numbers at current wage levels. The trend of real personal disposable income growth in the US is clearly downwards (see Figure 2.1). Adding workers or raising wages would not raise personal disposable income growth per capita – only unemployment.

This is not a cyclical situation, but a structural one that will persist until wages in emerging nations rise high enough to make lower-paid workers in industrial nations competitive with their counterparts in emerging nations. That is unlikely to happen for a long time for two reasons. First, union opposition to wage and benefit changes that

Figure 2.1 **Growth of real disposable personal income, 1947–2009 (%)**

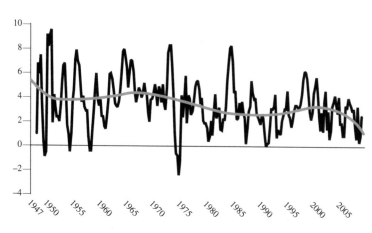

Source: Bureau of Economic Analysis

could make industrial nation workers competitive sooner is making them hard to implement. Second, the emerging nation threat to the higher-paid workers in industrial nations has ended the liberalisation of trade, a major factor in world growth in the post-war period.

Experience in the 1930s shows protectionism results in economic stagnation and deflation, but protectionism has political appeal. In spite of official protestations against it, the World Trade Organisation counted 47 trade restrictive measures in a four-month period ending in early 2009.[13] In addition, multiple failures to abide by World Trade Organisation rulings, the failed Doha round of negotiations, the recent spate of anti-dumping tariffs, reneging on agreements by imposing 'temporary' quotas on textiles and footwear from China and Vietnam, and job protection rulings and legislation show a rising tide of protectionism.

Today, protectionism also includes protecting domestic companies from foreign takeovers. The recent trend towards protecting industrial nation companies from takeovers by emerging nation companies shows the advantages of the former have evaporated. Protectionism will hurt developed nations more than emerging nations because the resulting slower world growth will increase the odds that developed nations will have to battle the investment decelerator unless they can find a way to restructure to increase multifactor productivity. Will the emerging nations' economic leadership be followed by financial leadership and will their currencies challenge the dollar's position as the global reserve currency?

The dollar has been much stronger than most people think

Emerging nations quadrupling the potential global labour force greatly enhanced the value of business assets – productive facilities to employ labour, the financial capital needed to build new plant and equipment, and the management capability to organise projects. Companies in industrial nations have these assets, and so benefited greatly from globalisation. Profits soared to record shares of national incomes and executive pay rose to obscene levels. Nevertheless, the gravitation of manufacturing, and even services, to emerging nations resulted in loss of confidence in the US dollar.

The broadest US dollar trade weighted index is, unsurprisingly, called the broad index. It consists of two sub-indices, the major currencies index (MCI) and the other important trading partners index (OITP – see Figure 2.2). The euro, Canadian dollar, yen and sterling constitute most of the MCI, which accounts for just over half of the broad index. The OITP constitutes just under half of the broad index. It includes the currencies of all nations not in the MCI that import more than 0.45% of US exports. The yuan and the Mexican peso constitute over half the OITP, about one-quarter of the broad index.

The MCI has traced an irregular downward trend since 1985

Figure 2.2 **US$ trade weighted indices, 1973–2009**

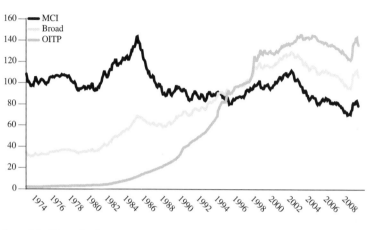

Source: Federal Reserve Board

while the explosive rise in the OITP index carried the broad index in a generally upward trend until October 2002. In spite of all the chatter about dollar weakness over the last three decades, the OITP is near its all-time high, so the dollar has been strong in a global context. The six years from 2002 to 2008 has been the only time the rise in the OITP did not more or less offset periodic falls in the MCI.

A big reason for the relative weakness in the MCI is that few of the OITP currencies are freely traded so they are easier to manipulate (which has meant to hold down in recent years), and their under-developed capital markets reduce their importance in financial markets. A second reason for the relative weakness in the MCI is that lack of confidence in the dollar encouraged nations to raise the proportion of euros (the biggest component of the MCI) in their reserves from 17% in 2001 to 27% in 2008. The following analysis concentrates on the MCI as it contains the most traded currencies and is affected far more than the OITP by what is happening in America.

Figure 2.3 **$ major currencies index and real effective exchange rate, 1973–2009**

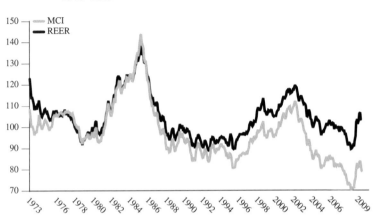

Source: Federal Reserve Board, Bank of International Setlements

Figure 2.3 shows that the fall in the real effective exchange rate (which deflates the currencies in the MCI index by their respective national inflation rates) of the dollar has been small and the dollar's current purchasing power relative to the currencies in the MCI significantly exceeds that of 30 years ago. Even though changes in the MCI generally track changes in the real effective exchange rate, the level of the MCI has fallen by 24 percentage points relative to the real effective exchange rate since 1985. Confidence in the dollar has dropped greatly, but that does not mean it is undervalued because it was far more overvalued in 1985 than the 4% shown in the figure.

European banks lent vast amounts of dollars to developing nations in the second half of the 1970s. Normally, loans by non-American banks to non-American borrowers do not significantly affect the dollar because repaying existing loans usually offsets the creation of new loans, but borrowing greatly exceeded repayments in that period. The excess of borrowing over repayment created dollars totally independent of US investment and trade flows because the borrowers converted the dollars into local currencies before spending them. This put downward pressure on the dollar that was totally unrelated to America and the MCI fell 15% in less than two years.

That was a big fall so soon after President Nixon shut the gold window in 1971 and ended the Bretton Woods Agreement of 1944. That agreement had put central banks in full control of national monetary policies, but continued the gold standard's fixed exchange regime. The various inflation rates that the differing national monetary policies produced were bound to destroy the fixed exchange rate aspect of Bretton Woods. America's desire to inflate faster than Europe finally did so, thereby unleashing a series of foreign exchange crises. The Latin American debt crisis was the first.

Mexico declared it could no longer service its debt in August 1982. Most Latin American loans were short term and commercial banks refused to refinance billions of dollars of loans to Latin American nations. Solvent borrowers needed dollars to repay their loans and banks with defaulted Mexican loans on their books needed dollars to service the liabilities stranded by the default, creating a big demand for dollars totally unrelated to usual American trade and investment flows. The currency soared far above a reasonable valuation. Assuming a 25% overvaluation in 1985 would make the dollar fairly valued now.

A similar cycle occurred recently. Most people investing in China believed the yuan would rise against the dollar, so few borrowed yuan if they could borrow dollars at a cheaper rate and convert the proceeds into yuan. China severely limits portfolio investment flows, both in and out. Dollar loans from Chinese banks converted into yuan explains how China's dollar reserves could grow far more than its trade surplus and net foreign direct investment inflows every year from 2001 to 2007. The excess dollars generated from loans by non-US banks to non-Americans put continuing downward pressure on the dollar, explaining the fall in the MCI relative to the

Figure 2.4 **US savings/investments versus trade deficits, 1947–2009, as % of GDP**

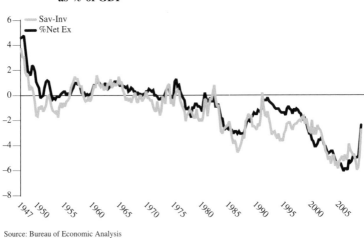

Source: Bureau of Economic Analysis

real effective exchange rate. The sudden Chinese slowdown in the second half of 2008 stopped the borrowing of dollars to spend in China, explaining the sudden rise in the dollar at that time against all expectations.

Dollar loans independent of US trade and investment flows explains changes in the dollar exchange rate much better than the difficulty in financing big US trade deficits cited by most analysts. Trade deficits are only one side of the foreign exchange equation; investment is the other. The US is a low investment nation, yet its domestic saving has met its investment needs in only one quarter in the past 25 years. Saving must equal investment, therefore the US must import saving to compensate for the deficiency of domestic saving – the root cause of the long string of US trade deficits (see Figure 2.4).

These trade deficits are virtually equal to current account deficits, so America's desire to consume imports relative to the foreign desire

46

to invest in the US is the trade dynamic in the foreign exchange value of the dollar. We cannot measure either desire directly but, in the absence of significant borrowing or repayment of dollar loans independent of American trade and investment flows, exchange rates give a good indication of their relative sizes.

Contrary to popular opinion, US current account deficits are not digging the US into a big hole. It has been the world's biggest debtor nation for years and its debts keep growing. However, US investments abroad are mostly investment in productive facilities and yield much more than foreign investments in the US, which are mostly fixed income. The differential in yield is so big that not only is the investment income part of the current account still in surplus, but the surplus has risen from $21 billion in 2000 to $128 billion in 2008. The save-and-export nations should be paying more attention to how the US invested its surplus savings when it had them.

Currency manipulation enabled vendor financing

The MCI and real effective trade weighted values of the dollar rose 19% and 20% respectively in the year to March 2009 (see Figure 2.3 on page 44). Even so, the massive financial bailout and economic stimulation packages enacted in the US have reawakened fears about the long-run value of the dollar and its status as a reserve currency. The US government seldom worries about the level of the dollar and the Federal Reserve has printed far more money than any other major central bank, except the Bank of England, as part of the bailout and stimulation packages.

Such massive printing of money should depress the value of the dollar in the long run, but some foreign holders of dollars have no choice but to invest in dollar assets. China has pegged the yuan to the dollar since 1995 (albeit more loosely since 2005) in an overtly mercantilist policy to maximise Chinese employment. Most nations competing with Chinese exports have also tied their currencies to the dollar – with varying degrees of rigidity – to retain competitiveness with China. Many oil-producing nations have done the same to keep their costs in line with their revenues.

This currency manipulation played a big part in creating the Eurasian savings glut, a gigantic vendor financing scheme whereby poor countries save to fund excess consumption in rich ones, first identified by Charles Dumas in 2004. This inversion of what is usually considered normal enabled Asia to greatly increase employment and wages by producing goods and services for consumption in the US and Europe. The dollars the US spends to fund current account deficits end up in exchange reserves of foreign central banks. Those with currencies tied to the dollar must invest the dollars they receive in US securities. This involuntary investment offsets the current account deficits with the nations manipulating their currencies, so neither the trade deficits nor the investments affect the level of the dollar.

Other central banks often keep most of their foreign exchange reserves in dollars because about 80% of world trade is priced in dollars. The flow of dollars back to the US has funded American current account deficits every year since 1981. Most of these dollars are invested in short- and medium-term fixed income assets. Unfortunately, the weak dollar and low American interest rates have created severe inflationary pressures in the nations that have pegged their currencies to the dollar. Kuwait revalued its currency in May 2007 and other Gulf states are wondering about maintaining their traditional links to the dollar.

Nations abandoning dollar pegs and denominating their trade in other currencies could weaken the dollar. Japan's banking system now allocates domestic saving efficiently and is in the best position to break the tie with the dollar. Kuwait changed the peg for the dinar from dollars to a basket of currencies and other oil producers may follow suit. Iran now receives non-dollar currencies for 'nearly all' its oil exports.

Furthermore, the massive size of US fiscal deficits and quantitative easing (see Chapter 3) are efforts to devalue the dollar – a clear violation of the obligations of a reserve currency. China is America's biggest creditor with $1.2 trillion in government and corporate bonds. It wants to protect itself from dollar devaluation and is demanding that Special Drawing Rights (SDRs) play an increasing role in the global monetary system. However, what that would accomplish other than a slight reduction of dollar exposure is not clear.

SDRs are a basket of currencies containing 44% dollars, 34% euros and 11% per cent each of yen and sterling. Current allocated reserves contain 64% dollars, 27% euros, 4% sterling, 3% yen and 2% other currencies. SDRs form part of national foreign exchange reserves and governments can use them as collateral for borrowing, so issuing SDRs could increase global money supply. International reserves totalled $6.7 trillion at the end of 2008, so the additional $250 billion SDRs that the G20 allocated in April 2009 is inconsequential. The International Monetary Fund (IMF) would have to issue SDRs continuously for them to play a significant role in the global money supply. This will not happen for a long time and currency reform or a global central bank is even further in the future. Even so, China will keep currency reform on the agenda.

Attacks on the dollar notwithstanding, it will not fall much, and it may rise further if other nations keep their currencies tied to it. This is likely as emerging nation banking systems need reform to enable them to collect savings and distribute them into productive assets more efficiently. Accumulating dollar reserves routes emerging nation savings through major financial centres, effecting the desired efficient allocation.

Deleverage could boost the dollar

American consumers reduced their saving and monetised assets, especially housing, to finance a 25-year spending binge. The annual household financial deficits after investment in housing from 1999 to 2008 were a bigger percentage of GDP and lasted longer than ever before. The corresponding explosion in household debt posed no problem while interest rates were falling, mortgage terms were becoming ever more favourable to borrowers and house prices were rising. The ratio of debt service to incomes remained fairly stable until 2004, and selling the house bailed out those who had borrowed too much.

The explosion in house prices and mortgage debt occurred because financial innovation had encouraged irresponsible lending and borrowing that trashed household balance sheets (see Chapter 3). Many American consumers were unable to pay their interest, and then falling house prices caused extensive negative equity. Tightening lending standards are aggravating credit problems, so consumer delinquencies and foreclosures are soaring. As a result, consumption and imports are slowing, which has begun the correction of the imbalances of saving and investment created by the Eurasian savings glut.

Other developed nations, such as the UK, Ireland and Spain, are following the US into a major housing, consumption and import correction, which should benefit the dollar. Increasing leverage created most of the dollar's problems. Gearing down would have reversed the negative influences on the dollar, but the US has implemented an unending series of quick-fix solutions designed to prevent gearing down. These are not only prolonging and worsening the credit problems, but are also undermining the value of the dollar. In addition, international challenges to US hegemony are hurting confidence in the dollar.

The end of the peace dividend

From the US perspective, the end of the Cold War in the 1990s created a 'peace dividend' that not only enhanced globalisation and prosperity, but also offered a chance to spread democracy and free markets as was done in Germany and Japan after the Second World War. The break-up of the Soviet Union left the US overwhelmingly powerful. Its economy is bigger than the next three (Japan, Germany and China) together, regardless of the method of measurement, and its military might is formidable. The US set out to reshape the world in its own image and this hubris is now eroding its position as a superpower.

The terrorist attacks on New York and Washington DC on 11 September 2001 (9/11) reversed the benign international atmosphere and began a new world order of increasing geopolitical tensions. The American response was to declare a 'War on Terror' – the first war ever to be launched without an identifiable enemy. The invasions of Afghanistan and Iraq polarised differences of opinion about the Middle East. A Washington Post/ABC News poll[14] showed the proportion of Americans who believe mainstream Islam promotes violence against non-believers rose from 14% in January 2002 to 32% in March 2006.

On the other side, more and more Arabs consider the 'War on Terror' to be a war on Islam and the failure to resolve the Israel-Palestine issue constitutes a constant irritant. The hope of resolving it in the near future seems remote and Iran's worrying nuclear programme continues. Terrorism is proliferating and is a great hindrance to the economic and political development of the entire region.

Resurgent Russia

As the US tried to reshape the world in its own image, Americans considered independence for Kosovo, the expansion of NATO and the deployment of US air force bases to Central Asia as logical results of the collapse of the Soviet Union. They called these incursions benign attempts to stabilise the region and integrate it into the global system, thus enhancing its prosperity and security. However, the US became so deeply embroiled in Afghanistan and Iraq after 9/11 that it had few resources to deploy on other challenges such as the instability in Pakistan – even though commitments remain to building its missile defence shield and tracking stations in Europe, extending democracy and free markets in former Soviet Union states, and expanding NATO to include Ukraine and Georgia.

Russia's perspective is, of course, the opposite of America's. Russia and the former Soviet Union underwent painful internal upheaval in the 1990s. What foreigners saw as reform Russians saw as a national catastrophe. They thought the US was taking advantage of their weakness to surround Russia with nations controlled by Americans through its military system, NATO.

The US dismissed Russia's concerns and continued to act in the belief that Russia would not challenge American interests. However, Russia was getting stronger, more united and better governed in the 2000s, and has asserted what it considers its interests in Chechnya and Georgia. Other nations have criticised the moves, but have done nothing more. In addition, Russia has refused to co-operate with the US on actions that could undermine the Iranian regime. If America wants Russia to co-operate on Iran, it will have to accept Russian interference in former Soviet Union countries.

Russia is increasingly likely to use cyber warfare, as it did with Georgia, and economic tactics, as it did with Ukraine, to regain the influence it desires over former Soviet Union nations. Russia cut off supplies to Ukraine in 2006 and 2009 to enforce its will. Europe depends heavily on Russian gas and oil, so cutting off gas to Ukraine reduced supplies to other European nations. To avoid the risk of having its supply of energy dictated by Russia, Europe must develop vast alternative sources of energy quickly. It is seeking to do so but the political leaning is towards windmills and biofuels, the advantages of which are doubtful, instead of energy sources that can produce the required amounts of energy more cost effectively such as clean coal, liquid natural gas and nuclear power.

China: the aspiring superpower

China's sphere of influence is expanding rapidly as its foreign policy provides investment and development, mainly in least developed nations. China is the natural leader of the communist bloc and has established good diplomatic and economic relationships with every 'rogue' state (including Iran with its 11% and 15% of the world's oil and gas reserves respectively) and many African states with natural resource wealth (Africa's oil reserves are triple those of Asia). China has already made several deals for Venezuelan oil, and will probably add Bolivia, Peru and Ecuador to its sphere of influence.

China is developing its strong and fast-growing economy as efficiently as the Asian tigers and has passed Germany to have the third biggest economy in dollar terms. In terms of purchasing power parity, it has been the second largest for a while and is approaching half the size of the US economy. China's trend growth rate is several times that of the US and the Chinese economy is stronger than the American. China is a major contributor to the Eurasian savings glut (see page 48) whereas the US is a borrow-and-spend nation depending on foreign saving to finance its investment and profligate government spending.

China is a relatively poor nation, yet high Chinese savings have not only maintained the highest level of investment ever seen, but also created the largest national foreign exchange reserve in the world. Global foreign exchange reserves soared from $2.1 trillion at the end of 2001 to $6.7 trillion at the end of 2008, a compound rate of growth of 18% a year. This rapid growth came from US current account deficits (see Figure 2.5) and nations in surplus accumulating dollars to keep their currencies artificially low. Three nations

Figure 2.5 **US current account, 1973–2008, in US$ (millions)**

Source: Bureau of Economic Analysis

– China, Japan and Russia – account for almost 40% of foreign exchange reserves and much of the rise since 2001.

The huge US current account deficits were necessary to import the saving needed to fund US domestic investment (see Figure 2.4 on page 46), creating a symbiotic relationship between the US and the surplus nations. A low savings rate means the US must consume more than it produces to import needed saving; the surplus nations must export to the US to employ the surplus labour arising from their lack of domestic demand. This symbiotic relationship is causing ultimately unsustainable global imbalances.

The investment of the reserves amassed by the save-and-export nations caused a mounting interest rate burden in the borrow-and-spend nations. Funding both the excess consumption and the interest payable on the rising debt burden meant their debt had to grow faster than their incomes, so asset prices had to keep rising and/or interest rates had to keep falling. Interest rates stopped falling in 2003, the serial asset booms ended in 2006 and the credit bubble burst in 2007. Consumers in the borrow-and-spend nations do not have the savings or income growth to service the growing debt loads needed to maintain the symbiotic relationship with the surplus nations, so the relationship is breaking down.

China is the biggest source of funding for US debt. This could give it a measure of power over the superpower, but China's mercantilist policies make that power illusory. Even so, China believes this is the first step to its long-term goal of gaining superpower status, but its reluctance to give up the save-and-export model of growth is frustrating its ambitions.

What holds China back from becoming a superpower

The end of the credit bubble is slowing growth in the borrow-and-spend nations to a crawl, but save-and-export nations can maintain trend growth by substituting domestic demand for the lost export sales. However, Chinese policymakers seem to be clinging to the save-and-export model that has served them so well in the past. They stopped the rise in the yuan in response to the slowing in the growth of exports. This was counterproductive because the rising yuan not only raised China's stature in global politics and markets, but also was reducing the cost of imports and so helping to create the needed domestic demand.

In addition, the relative price of food (see Chapter 1) makes inflation a more serious problem in poor nations, such as China, as food is a much bigger component of household purchases. Moreover, China uses resources only half as efficiently as the US. Rising commodity prices increased input costs while competition in export markets limited the rise in output prices. The return on assets after depreciation has therefore been low. The rising yuan was boosting the paltry return on investment by lowering import costs. Slowing export markets and a rising yuan are precisely what China needs to accomplish two necessary policy objectives at the same time – to lower inflation and to stimulate domestic demand. And a rising proportion of domestic sales could improve profit margins.

China's combination of communist politics and liberal economics can survive only as long as people expect economic growth to raise their living standards. Insufficient improvement will frustrate ambitions and encourage unrest. As a result of the one-child policy, the number of unattached males is rising and could reach 33 million by 2020. The few other examples in history in which sex ratios became this imbalanced – third-century Rome, for example, or the American western frontier in the mid-19th century – tended to be highly volatile and violent.[15] A ratio of 129 males to 100 females was the prime cause of the Nien Rebellion in the 1850s.[16] The ratio in Hunan Province in south central China is now 137:100 and rising.

China's failure to embrace this opportunity to replace exports with domestic demand will make adjustment to the slow growth in North America and Europe much more disruptive to both China and the rest of the world. The slowdown in 2008 induced the government to take a big backward step and replace market-based investment with investment in infrastructure through state-owned enterprises. This will slow China's growth by impairing its ability to raise the value-added component of its output, a key factor in its meteoric growth.

The increasing volatility of economic growth resulting from high levels of investment is one factor impeding China's ambitions to become a superpower. Investment rises and falls faster than the economy as a whole. The greater the proportion of investment in GDP the more volatile GDP should be in the long run. However, Chinese economic statistics have not demonstrated this volatility. One explanation is that China's comparative advantage has been so great that demand for its products has been high enough to produce consistent maximum growth; the other is that the Chinese manipulate their figures so they show what the authorities want them to show. Both probably played a part in the 'Chinese miracle'.

However, China's comparative advantage is ebbing, export growth is slowing and the proportion of investment has begun to fall, initiating a significant slowdown. Official figures do not show its true extent, but financial markets have felt its full force. Much of China's industry is financed by debt and the Chinese financial system is not as solid as it looks. The bulk of the loans are to state-owned enterprises, which are, almost by definition, bad credit risks. The fall of over 70% in the Shanghai stock market from the 2007 peak to the 2008 low and the 95% drop in the Baltic Dry Index of shipping in 2008 showed that the Chinese economy had big problems. Then exports fell sharply in late 2008 and early 2009.

Recovery may have begun in 2009, but it is still too early to assess the scale of the damage. In late 2008, the government estimated $600 billion of Chinese loans were paying neither principal nor interest, but Stratfor, a world leader in global intelligence, placed the figure closer to $1.1 trillion, about 40% of the country's nominal GDP. Recurrent banking crises have plagued many nations. Japan's 'lost decade' started when non-performing loans reached about 20% of GDP, so China faces severe banking problems even if the government figures are the more accurate. The slowdown will increase the amount of bad loans to be written off to intolerable levels. The timing of the write-offs is uncertain, but a major banking crisis is probable, as are political problems in other countries.

Other factors that hinder China's chances of attaining superpower status include lingering corruption at the regional government level; banks' lack of skills in assessing the creditworthiness of borrowers; demographic trends (if its birth rates remain unchanged, China will join the ranks of Japan, Germany, Russia, Italy and Spain – countries that stand to lose 20–30% of their populations over the next 50 years[17]); inadequate supplies of clean water (see Chapter 1); and aspects of its foreign policy – that China's policy of foreign investment includes selling arms to repressive regimes, such as Sudan, and keeping dictators like Robert Mugabe afloat with loans may rebound on it when the political landscape changes.

America's status as sole superpower is under threat

EU politicians want to create a United States of Europe superpower that will take over from the US as the dominant superpower. Their chances of succeeding in the near future are slim. American hegemony grew out of its traditions of low taxation, freedom and democracy. US governments tax and spend far less than EU governments, so America enjoys much stronger growth. The American stress on equality of opportunity frees everyone to do the best they can. The European stress on equality of outcome saps initiative and limits innovation.

Maintaining superpower status requires sensible domestic and foreign policies as well as a strong economy. The US has neither, even though, measured in dollars, the American economy was bigger than the next four nations together in 2007 and its water supplies exceed of those most nations. Its military might is unmatched and its location between Europe and Asia gives it a command of both the transatlantic and transpacific trade routes. The US will remain the sole superpower for some time, but its position is becoming weaker.

The end of the credit cycle and the tax increases to pay the interest on its burgeoning debts will slow US trend growth to a snail's pace for the foreseeable future. Chinese output should gain ground on US output even faster than in the past. Purchasing power parity (PPP) is a better indicator of economic power than dollar-based GDP. The US economy was about twice as big as China's in PPP terms in 2007, and according to World Bank data it will be less than 30% larger than China's in 2013.

Worse, the US economy is no longer strong. Strong economies

generate high rates of saving to enable high rates of investment, as America's did in the past. US net saving (gross saving less the consumption of fixed capital) was over 10% of GDP until the 1970s, enough to fund the desired domestic productive facilities with a surplus for investment abroad. US saving has been declining since the early 1970s. Exportable surplus saving disappeared in the early 1980s and net saving was negative (less than capital consumption) in 2008. Investment in America depends on the saving of foreign nations, so the country is beholden to those nations. By contrast, China's mercantilism depends on exports to the US – but that may change.

China designed its new five-year plan to raise domestic consumption at the expense of exports and to spread the wealth to rural areas, by government spending if need be. Chinese savings rates should fall, even though implementing this plan has been slow. Japan's ageing and falling population will save less as time goes on. Oil prices have hit a cyclical high, and probably a structural high (see Chapter 1), so the savings of oil exporters should fall too. The volume of internationally traded saving will fall. US imports of foreign saving, investment and output growth will be correspondingly lower, reducing its ability to continue its massive military spending.

A development that would have far-reaching consequences would be if China, with its manufacturing capabilities, and Russia, with its abundant natural resources, put aside their differences and learned to trust each other. A Sino-Russian bloc could challenge US hegemony, in part through its ability to restrict energy supplies to developed nations. Even so, it is unlikely that a Sino-Russian bloc could supersede NATO.

Emerging nations' impact on commodities

The rapid growth of emerging nations has spurred global competition for long-term supplies of commodities. Commodity prices, especially of energy, precious metals and base metals, have become even more volatile than usual as a result of terrorist or governmental action disrupting supplies.

Commodity prices have risen and fallen for centuries. The rises and falls are usually 20–30 years long, so successive peaks and troughs are 50–60 years apart. Commodity price indices peaked in 1974 and fell for a quarter of a century to double troughs in 1999 and 2001. History suggests that we are less than halfway through a normal 20+ year rise in commodity prices, the massive correction in 2008 notwithstanding. Previous commodity price booms led to increasing geopolitical tensions because of rising international competition to gain access to ever scarcer resources. Today's competition to gain control of resources and attempts to sabotage or divert supplies is nothing new, but part of an age-old pattern.

Oil has attracted the most competition and terrorist attacks because most people fear Hubbert's Peak (the theory that world oil production is nearing a peak and will soon decline) is true. Asian demand has been soaring, so most people expect supplies of oil will fall below demand, forcing prices ever higher. They fear the higher oil prices will slow growth, particularly in nations lacking secure sources. Strongly rising prices for the future delivery of commodities relative to their spot prices began an international competition for resources, and that competition is raising geopolitical tensions.

Much of the tension concerns the former Soviet Union and the Middle East, which together contain about three-quarters of the world's natural gas reserves. Russia tried to cut off gas exports to Ukraine in 2007 and the supply to western Europe fell sharply. This could have created an international incident, had it lasted longer, but it only sparked a European desire to secure alternative gas supplies. The replay in 2009 had little effect on western Europe.

Many emerging nations, including China and India, subsidise domestic energy usage. This minimises conservation, so they are even more anxious than the US and Europe to secure energy supplies. They not only compete for resources in stable areas, but also befriend countries containing resources, especially in the Middle East and Africa, that the OECD either ignores or blacklists. Success in gaining access to resources in such nations is giving Asia a big competitive advantage in addition to cheap labour.

A riskier world

Rising geopolitical tensions are adding to financial risks, making effective evaluation of risk an ever higher priority. As a result, international reserves and capital flows have begun to fall, especially into Russia. This is adding to the demand deflationary effects of the end of the credit cycle and tightening lending standards (see Chapters 3 and 4). The rising geopolitical tensions are also highlighting the ineffectiveness of the world's debating forums.

The belief that the UN would bring world peace has never been realised as powerful nations sidestep it and several nations are in breach of its resolutions. The G8 and the G20 control the policies of the international financial institutions such as the IMF and the World Bank. The policies they impose may suit developed nations, but these are seldom appropriate for the less and least developed nations in which they are being applied.

The world's population has become increasingly mobile, so the chances for international misunderstandings have multiplied. The UN has more than twice as many member nations as there were countries in the world in 1913, so increasing globalisation needs a continuous breakdown of artificial barriers to minimise geopolitical tensions.

Conclusion

Output, productivity and living standards should rise faster in emerging nations than in industrial nations throughout the forecast period, but only if the surplus nations raise domestic consumption enough to offset much of the decline in their export markets. Little evidence has emerged as yet to show they will do so before they face demographic problems of their own that will make replacing lost exports impossible. Moreover, as we saw in Chapter 1, the rising costs of food and energy are likely to be substantial drags on world growth, so it will probably slow significantly.

Financial activity is not gravitating to emerging nations as fast as industrial activity because their banking systems remain less able to channel national saving into productive facilities efficiently. With help from industrial nation bankers, banking systems in less developed nations are becoming more efficient, albeit more accident-prone.

Geopolitical tensions will continue to rise and increase risk as a result of competition for resources. Many developed nation governments are becoming ever more authoritarian in the name of national security. Adding resources to national security is hindering economic growth and the rise in living standards, especially in developed nations.

Refusal to compromise has always led to more misunderstandings and conflict as population mobility rose. Unfortunately, the world's record on resolving conflicts remains abysmal. The efforts of the international financial institutions have been so futile that more and more people, even from within the agencies themselves, are demanding that the UN, World Bank and other international agencies be either thoroughly reformed or abolished.

3

Is inflation inevitable?

Under the now defunct gold standard, bank reserves were held in gold. As the world's supply of gold grows extremely slowly, the gold standard strictly limited the growth of bank reserves and money – except in Tudor times when inflows of bullion from the New World more than trebled prices. That was the only period of sustained inflation between the fall of Rome and the Second World War. In 1600 £3 6s 2d was required to buy what £1 had bought in 1525.[18] The flow of gold into Europe shrank after the defeat of the Spanish Armada and prices rose only sporadically for more than three centuries thereafter. In 1933 it took only £2 15s 6d to buy what £1 had bought in 1600.

Limiting the growth of money restricted credit growth too, so only the better credits could borrow. The gold standard disallowed printing money, so governments were seldom among the better credits, restricting government spending to current revenues. After the First World War, ambitious governments progressively removed limits to the creation of money and credit until the Bretton Woods Agreement of 1944 created universal fiat money by giving governments and central banks complete control of national monetary policies.

Fiat money unleashed the biggest inflation in Europe and North America since the fall of Rome. Central banks increased bank reserves and money supplies far too quickly, so government spending and inflation soared. In 2007 £50.88 was required to buy what

£1 had bought in 1933. Central bank inflation was more than 15 times more virulent than the inflation resulting from the inflow of gold from the New World. A similar, but much less rampant, pattern occurred in America. In 1933 $1.46 bought what $1 had bought in 1665; in 2007 $16.00 was needed to buy what $1 bought in 1933.[19]

Inflation is always and everywhere a monetary phenomenon. The current US money supply series began in 1959. M2 has grown 6.9% a year since 1959 and real GDP has grown 3.3%. The difference is 3.6% a year and the GDP deflator grew by 3.7% a year. Central banks create inflation by expanding their balance sheets too rapidly. The monetary base is the main source of the growth in the supply of money and is virtually identical to the central bank's liabilities. The changes in the total of comparable broad money supplies in the three largest currency blocs followed the changes in the sum of their monetary bases until September 2008 – even though financial deregulation and innovation had created a bewildering array of new investment instruments (see Figure 3.1). Government resistance to credit liquidation created a short anomaly thereafter.

Arguably, changes in the monetary base explained more than half the changes in broad money growth in the three blocs up to September 2008. Capital now flows across borders relatively freely in search of higher interest rates, so an international monetary base denotes international money growth better than a national monetary base denotes national money growth. Arbitrageurs borrow money in nations with excessive monetary base growth and low interest rates and invest it in nations with higher interest rates. As we will see later, these global money flows have created serious economic imbalances.

Central banks have not controlled the monetary base

Central banks control short-term interest rates in order to keep

Figure 3.1 **Growth in monetary base and money supply, 2000–09**

Source: Lombard Street Research

inflation at acceptable levels. Their daily operations to keep interest rates at their targets affect their balance sheets and the monetary
base. Central banks create inflation because their interest rate targets
are usually too low, so they must keep increasing their assets and
liabilities, known as printing money, to keep policy interest rates
down to the targeted level. 'Printing money' was the gold standard
term for monetary stimulation. Modern, aggressive monetary stimulation is called 'quantitative easing' but the terms are essentially syn-
onymous. Quantitative easing is being presented as a new tool being
used only in exceptional circumstances, but it is as old as monetary
policy itself.

Changes in the size of the central bank balance sheet cause
the changes in the monetary base. Controlling the monetary base,
thereby limiting money growth to a non-inflationary level over time,
is easy, at least in theory. Gold limited the global monetary base
and money supply for centuries, but few if any central banks have

targeted the growth of their balance sheets. Several have targeted one or more money supply measures but failed to achieve their targets. The Fed (the US Federal Reserve), for example, targeted M1 growth from 1975 to 1986 and M2 growth from 1975 to 1993, but the targets had little credibility, as they were seldom met. Moreover, studies show the Fed had desired most of the deviation from the targets. The Fed wanted the US money supply to grow too quickly before, during and after the targets, for three reasons:

- Its remit includes encouraging optimum growth in output and employment. This is far more important to politicians than maintaining the value of the currency, so they keep pressuring the Fed to keep interest rates low enough to stimulate faster growth – even when growth is above its sustainable trend.
- It fears the US financial system is vulnerable to systemic failure and deflation. The Fed injected huge amounts of liquidity into the financial system to avoid escalating defaults when the Penn Central Railroad failed in 1970, and has done the same in every significant credit incident since.
- It believes deflation is a far greater threat than inflation, so it wants to avoid deflation at all costs.

Thus the Fed always errs on the side of excess money growth in slow growth periods and insufficient removal of excess liquidity in booms. The US money supply has grown far more rapidly than necessary to maintain optimal growth in output since the Second World War. The excess growth caused rising inflation until the early 1980s. The Fed under Paul Volcker began a credit crunch in 1979 that reversed the direction of inflation and many other central banks adopted inflation targets thereafter. This seemed to be a successful policy as inflation rates kept falling, but the success was more apparent than real.

Inflation shifted from goods and services to assets

Competition from Asia reduced the rates of growth in output in developed nations after the credit crunch in the early 1980s. Even so, rapidly falling interest rates kept credit growing at the same 9% rate as before the credit crunch because fiat money bestows unlimited ability to create debt. The rate of growth of productive investment fell in America and Europe, so ever more debt funded purchases of assets rather than plant and equipment. As a result, the prices of stocks, bonds, commodities, real estate, art, antiques, memorabilia and so on inflated into bubbles.

Most of the lending after the credit crunch in the early 1980s occurred outside the regulated banking system (see Figure 3.2), so central banks could do little to curb the growth in debt short of raising interest rates to levels that would have incurred slowdowns or recessions. They would have been severely criticised for doing so. Most people believe rising asset prices create real wealth and falling asset prices destroy it. This is nonsense: only new investment in buildings and equipment and the discovery of natural resources add to a nation's real wealth. Higher asset prices cannot add to real wealth because they do not create anything that did not exist before.

But they do give the owners of the assets more buying power, and the added purchases may stimulate more investment and exploration for natural resources, which would add to real wealth. However, fiat money does not bestow unlimited ability to pay interest and the inability to pay the interest on debts ultimately limits lending. The added purchasing power is reversed when debt reaches its limit. It is now clear that the private sector in America, Britain and other nations has exceeded the limit of its ability to pay interest.

Similarly, only the obsolescence or destruction of buildings and equipment and the consumption of natural resources that are not replaceable deplete a nation's real wealth. Lower asset prices do not destroy real wealth, but they do reduce the buying power of those

Figure 3.2 **US debt and broad money, 1958–2008, as % of GDP**

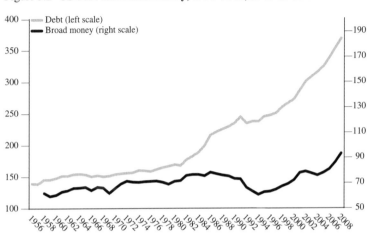

Source: Federal Reserve Board; Lombard Street Research

who own the assets. Decreased demand may lower investment and reduce exploration for natural resources enough to allow depreciation and depletion to diminish real wealth. The diminutions are reversed when asset prices stop falling and start rising. So how did the credit bubble develop?

Debt is the main counterpart to money. Debt and money grew at about the same rate until the early 1980s when the biggest disintermediation of lending in history started. Unbeknown to anyone at the time, financial deregulation and innovation together with rising US current account deficits were transforming the relative roles of money and credit. The credit crunch in the early 1980s had wreaked havoc among American commercial and savings banks. Bank failures reduced the broad money to GDP ratio for almost a decade (Figure 3.2). That ratio began to rise again in the mid-1990s, and just regained the 1959–86 trend in 2008. Less excess money being created by the Fed reduced the rates of inflation in incomes and goods and services – with a lot of help from the competition generated by a couple of billion Asian workers joining the global workforce.

Interest rates fell greatly from the 1981 highs as a result of rising capital inflows (the counterpart of the rising current account deficits) and financial innovations that took advantage of the deregulation that began in 1978. This expanded markets for debt outside a banking system that had been greatly weakened by the credit crunch and could not meet its share of the demand for credit, which grew an average of 9% a year both before and after the credit crunch. Thus began the greatest disintermediation of debt in history, which misallocated capital into a huge credit bubble. Disintermediation and financial innovation turned many non-bank financial institutions (shadow banks) into a parallel banking system that performed most of the functions of commercial banks, but were free from many of the restrictions on the latter.

Financial innovation greatly increased risk

The most important financial innovations were structured finance, credit insurance and hedging for financial instruments. Structured finance involves securitisation, which began in the early 1970s with the creation of asset-backed securities (ABS) – debt collateralised by the cash flow from a specified pool of underlying assets that otherwise might be highly illiquid. The asset pools can consist of any type of receivable such as commercial and residential mortgages, auto loans, credit card payments, student loans, royalty payments, aircraft leases and movie revenue. The main disadvantage of securitisation is its greater cost, so it is not cost effective for small and medium-sized borrowings.

Three characteristics define securitised instruments:

• pooling of assets (either cash-based or synthetically created);

- de-linking the credit risk of the collateral asset pool from the credit risk of the originator, usually through a special purpose vehicle (SPV);
- a trust that either passes the cash flow from the assets directly to investors or creates different tranches with different risks and returns.

The original purpose of securitisation was to reduce borrowing costs by giving investors the security of high-quality assets as well as some margin. Ford Motor's credit rating was downgraded to junk, but its senior automobile-backed securities continued to be rated AAA because of the strength of the underlying collateral and over-collateralisation. Other securities of companies that securitise their best assets should be downgraded accordingly, because securitisation does not reduce the total risk incurred in a company's operations, but that is seldom done.

Levered ABS called collateralised debt obligations (CDO) alter the risk profiles of securitised loans even more. Trust indentures for CDO package the cash flows into tranches with different levels of risk and return according to market demand. Figure 3.3 shows the flow of payments from the mortgagors to the investors into either ABS or CDO. ABS debt has high ratings. Tranching into classes with different risk/return profiles widens the market for securitisation by appealing to investors with different risk appetites. The senior bonds have first claim on cash flows, and are usually rated AAA to A; mezzanine bonds have a subordinate claim on cash flows and are usually rated BBB to B. The equity class is the most junior, unrated, and receives the residual proceeds of the collateral – but also absorbs the initial losses.

Tranching requires detailed documentation to ensure that the desired characteristics, such as the seniority ordering the various tranches, will be delivered under all plausible scenarios. One recommended division was 91% senior classes, 5% mezzanine classes and

Figure 3.3 **Payment flow from mortgagor to investor**

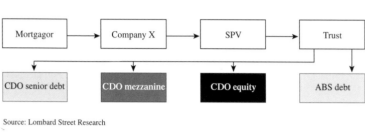

Source: Lombard Street Research

4% equity. The high risk of the equity class has led to allegations of mis-selling and commentators have called it 'toxic waste'. The originator of the loans or the underwriter of the securities issued under the trust often retains the equity, because the originator was subject to the losses before the securitisation and the underwriter understands the risks. The mezzanine class absorbs any further losses after the equity is gone until it too is exhausted. This class is usually the least attractive on a risk-adjusted basis and often ends up in the hands of investors who do not understand the risks.

The junior classes exist to insulate the senior classes from the default risk of the underlying asset pool. Under adverse circumstances, the senior classes absorb losses in order of seniority. CDO structures always create one or more classes of securities rated higher than the average of the underlying asset pool. Underwriters may call the most senior class 'super senior' but rating agencies do not recognise the designation.

Like ABS, CDO is a generic term that includes structures collateralised by bonds, loans, ABS, commercial real estate and other CDO securities (CDO^2 and CDO^3 – particularly difficult vehicles to model because of the possible repetition of exposures in the underlying assets). One aim of structured finance was to transfer credit risk, but the originators of loans do not have to sell them to transfer the credit risk. Instead, they can buy credit default swaps (CDS),

Figure 3.4 **Synthetic CDO risk profile**

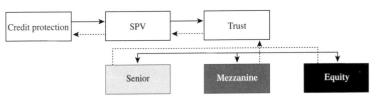

Source: Lombard Street Research

contracts that sell insurance on a specific security or basket of loans. CDS buyers transfer the credit risk to the CDS sellers. Synthetic CDO securitise cash flows from derivatives such as CDS rather than assets. The details of synthetic CDO can vary but the essential risk profile of those based on CDS is shown in Figure 3.4. Ratings are the same as for cash CDO.

The inherent risks in cash and in synthetic CDO are almost the same if the buyers of the credit protection own the assets they insure. In the event of default, CDS sellers pay the buyers the face value of the debt less the amount recovered, and so lose exactly what they would have had they invested in cash CDO. But credit protection buyers do not have to own the assets they insure, and neither the buyers nor the sellers need to inform the borrower of their activities. All that is required is willing buyers and sellers of credit protection on the reference debt.

The synthetic CDO market was huge, constituting over 90% of the CDO in Europe and about half of those in the US. Many were formed from large pools (usually 100 names) of CDS that were created for the sole purpose of forming a CDO. Thus the total of the CDS outstanding usually exceeds the total of the debt they insure many times over. The excess is speculation by both buyers and sellers. Credit insurance sellers were much more anxious than buyers, so premiums on CDS fell for several years to an all-time low and were almost the same for industrial and high-tech companies as for pharmaceutical firms and utilities in 2007.

Moreover, premiums on ten-year CDS fell markedly relative to one-year CDS as investors apparently assumed the credit cycle would not turn for at least a decade – just before the sub-prime mortgage fiasco hit the headlines. Then lending standards tightened and CDS premiums soared, widening the credit spreads on cash bonds and loans. Meanwhile the huge amounts of CDS outstanding multiplied the problems of the sub-prime mortgage lenders, raising fears of both contagion and the future solvency of CDS sellers.

Secondary market trading in ABS is similar to corporate bond trading. Most of it is done in over-the-counter markets and no measures of trading volume are publicly available. However, few CDO are liquid because they are not standardised. Investors must evaluate the individual credits, different structures, maturity profiles, credit enhancements and other features of a CDO before trading it. As a result, secondary trading is so light that prices are usually determined by computer models.

Computer model pricing has led to significant problems. Lenders securitise cash flows to enjoy most of the benefits of lending money without bearing the credit risk. They earn fees from originating the loans and continuing to service them throughout their life. Selling loans to SPV reduces the risk-weighted assets of the originators, allowing them to originate still more loans. The debt holders, not the loan originators, suffer the losses from defaulted loans in securitised pools, so quantity of lending became much more profitable than quality of lending. Loan quality plummeted as a result. This is an important point and we will return to it later.

Investors flocked to securitisations because they gave higher rates of return on highly rated assets. There was a dearth of highly rated bonds, but securitisations created large quantities of AAA, AA and A rated debt that yielded more than comparably rated corporate or sovereign bonds. The higher yields compensated for risks inherent in ABS, such as amortisation risk. The principal amount borrowed is paid back gradually over the specified term of the debt, rather than in one lump sum at maturity. The possible rate of prepayment can vary widely on the loans underlying most ABS. For example, interest rate changes affect the prepayment rates on some underlying loans, especially mortgages. All cash CDO are subject to prepayment risk when interest rates are falling.

Structured finance divorced the credit risk inherent in the loans from the credit risk of the originators of the loans. Credit insurance divorced the credit risk inherent in financial assets from their market risk. Hedging divorced the market risk of assets from the credit risk. This greater ability to isolate risks led to a much higher use of leverage.

The only risks asset owners could not lay off were liquidity risk and counterparty risk. Both are endogenous, that is, dependent on how the players in the market react to events in the market. Mathematicians are in charge of risk assessment. The probabilities of endogenous risks cannot be modelled in the same way as external risks because they are subjective, not objective. Mathematicians cannot calculate subjective risks, so they basically ignore them. A continuous flow of funds from current account surplus nations to current account deficit nations stabilised financial markets. That stability encouraged lenders and borrowers to lever their balance sheets more than ever before.

Shadow banks could gear up more than commercial banks and the higher gearing let them shave lending margins. Competition from the shadow banks together with the capital regulations imposed on commercial banks in the late 1980s forced them to change their business models. They reduced their loan ratios by selling loans to shadow banks and reduced their liquidity ratios by greatly increasing their holdings of 'other securities', both on and off their balance sheets. Neither commercial banks nor shadow banks realised how much gearing up their balance sheets had multiplied liquidity risk, so they had no viable exit strategies. Predictably, many got caught in a vicious liquidity squeeze when adverse market conditions occurred.

Few people recognised that structured finance had multiplied credit risk and rising leverage had multiplied the endogenous risks at the same time. Worse, the explosion in the amounts of derivatives outstanding added hugely to the risks most people were blithely ignoring.

Derivatives added greatly to the problems

Many people took great comfort from the rapid growth of derivatives because they spread risk widely, reducing each individual's risk. That comfort was misplaced because they increased total collective risk. The amount that could be settled in kind limited the amount of derivatives outstanding until the introduction of cash settlement ended that limit. Now, the amount of derivatives outstanding is usually many times the amount of the underlying commodity or security, and many derivatives are based on other derivatives, not commodities or securities. This has raised the collective risk from derivatives geometrically.

Derivatives greatly exceeded their legitimate hedging functions and created a risk seeker's paradise, so the outstanding amounts exploded in the liquidity-induced euphoria. Many of these derivatives were so complex few understood the risks they entailed. This, as well as multiple exposures to the same credits, plummeting lending standards due to structured finance and soaring leverage, created so much collective risk that problems in US sub-prime mortgages (a mere $1 trillion asset class) initiated a worldwide banking crisis in which losses to financial institutions are already estimated to exceed $4 trillion.

Warren Buffett called derivatives 'a ticking financial time bomb' because the rise in collective risk is an increase in systemic risk.

Derivative pricing models caused catastrophic losses by underesti-mating both the probability defaults and the amount of correlation between financial markets.

The combination of structured finance and derivatives created the highest ever debt to GDP ratios and interest costs relative to incomes. Moreover, all that debt and credit risk had been levered many times higher than ever before, especially through compound derivatives that multiplied potential losses on the same underlying credits. That entire mountain of dodgy debt imploded into what will probably become the biggest banking crisis in history. Governments are desperately trying to ward off a credit contraction, but they will ultimately fail because of the credit cycle that has caused spiralling debt to GDP ratios since the Second World War ended.

The three stages of the credit cycle

Creditworthiness falls when total debt outstanding rises faster than nominal GDP. In the 1970s, an American economist, Hyman Minsky, described the three stages of the credit cycle caused by debt rising faster than GDP. The 1940–2007 credit cycle evolved and ended just as he predicted. Each stage is a mini cycle that ends in credit prob-lems that morph into the next stage.

In the first stage, rising debts incur bigger interest payments, but much of the additional borrowing funds investment to expand pro-duction. Revenues from the added production are sufficient to pay the interest and repay the principal. Such debt is self-liquidating and so will never pose economic problems. Borrowers intend to repay their debts in full, so moral hazard and defaults are inconsequential until lenders and borrowers start to forget their disciplines. The first stage of the current cycle started in the Second World War. The Penn Central default in 1970 began the credit crunch that morphed into the second stage.

Lending standards are lower in the second stage, which in this cycle started in the 1980s. Most borrowers can service only interest payments out of their cash flows, so they need liquid capital markets to let them roll over the principal of their debts. Inability to repay debt from cash flow turns debt into a cheap form of equity. Lenders take equity risks, but they do not get equity returns. Also, borrowing is less for the construction of productive facilities and more for the purchase of assets. Debt used to buy assets adds nothing to output, so interest costs become ever heavier burdens on incomes. Only future income or selling assets can pay interest and repay principal on such debt, so it is not self-liquidating and can cause big problems as the productivity of debt falls. An additional $1 of debt added only 15 cents to output in 2008, down from 85 cents in 1966.

In the second stage, borrowers worry only about how much more they can borrow, never about repaying their debts, so default rates soar if liquidity dries up. A drop in liquidity caused soaring defaults in 2001–02 which ended the second stage of the credit cycle. It also panicked officials into excessive easing much too far into the recovery and bailing out companies 'too big to fail', both of which created moral hazard. The bailouts encouraged lending institutions to believe they could make risky loans that would pay handsomely if the investment turned out well, but they would not have to fully pay for the losses if the investment turned out badly.

Moral hazard also encouraged irresponsible lending and borrowing in the third stage of the credit cycle. Most borrowers tried to maximise debt and minimise equity and many could not pay interest from their cash flows. Lenders assumed the prices of collateralised assets would always rise and so provide security for their loans if the lenders failed to pay the interest. Minsky called this pyramid debt. Continuously rising asset prices required continuously rising debt, which in turn needed a continuous supply of borrowers. Lending standards had to keep falling to attract a sufficient supply of borrowers – and they hit rock bottom with 'ninja' mortgages where applicants had no verifiable income, job or assets.

Lending standards could drop no further, so mortgage debt could no longer grow rapidly enough to support rising house prices. House prices fell, the credit bubble burst and the third stage of the credit cycle ended.

The banking crisis ending the first stage of this credit cycle was limited to credit markets for two reasons. First, saving provided the capital required for investment and household balance sheets provided a stable base for the ensuing credit expansion. Saving provides equity, a completely safe form of capitalisation because it does not involve a future liability. Individuals and businesses with high levels of equity do not default if adverse conditions strike – regardless of how unexpectedly. Second, leverage outside the banking system was low, so bank failures had almost no secondary effects. Losses to investors outside the banking system were minuscule.

The banking crisis at the end of the second stage affected all financial markets. Household saving was much lower, household balance sheets were more fragile and leverage outside the banking system was much higher. Those who borrow excessively often default, so bankruptcies and losses outside the banking system were vastly higher than in the previous crisis.

A 'Minsky moment' occurs at the end of the third stage of the credit cycle. It bursts the credit bubble, ends the cycle of credit growing faster than output and affects the whole developed world. The entire financial structure changes drastically as a result. The stock market crash in late October 1929 was the Minsky moment in the last major credit cycle because rising stock prices had been supporting the debt pyramid. Once the stock market started falling, the credit structure was bound to implode sooner or later. It did so in early 1930.

The Minsky moment in this cycle was in 2006 when house prices started to fall. Rising house prices had supported the debt pyramid, so falling house prices caused soaring delinquencies and foreclosures. At the time, household saving was virtually non-existent and the entire financial structure more levered than ever before. The high leverage in household balance sheets means consumers will not save us this time.

Growth has been weaker than the official figures indicate. The US has used hedonic pricing in its inflation indices for several years to adjust prices for the continuing quality improvements in goods and services. For example, if the price of a model of digital camera rose from $169.99 to $199.99, consumers would experience 18% inflation. However, that price rise would not appear in the inflation figures if the statisticians felt the camera had become more 'useable' in the interim. If they calculated it was now, say, 30% more usable, they would adjust its former price to $169.99 × 1.3 = $220.99. The actual cost of the camera was then $21 less than their adjusted price, so its price would go into the inflation index as a *drop* of 9.5%.

Many consumers have no interest in many of the additional features and would prefer to buy a stripped down version for less money. This means US inflation statistics now understate inflation and so overstate both output and productivity. Other major nations have followed the US lead in using hedonic pricing to calculate inflation. The price of gold began to rise in all major currencies soon after hedonic pricing came into general use, indicating that hedonic pricing (and so inflation, GDP and productivity numbers) is worthless. Unemployment figures do not reflect the real weakness in growth because they have received similar makeovers. In fact, government figures are now so highly massaged that historical comparisons are becoming ever more meaningless.

However, we can be sure that falling real incomes, lack of saving and trashed household balance sheets mean that consumers will not be able to save us from a long period of below-trend growth. People thought US households were in great financial shape in 2006 because the market value of their assets was about five times their liabilities. That figure looked impressive, but it was down by two-thirds from 15 times liabilities 50 years previously in spite of the massive increase in the prices of their assets in the interim.

Defaults occur because of an inability to pay on time, so the availability of liquid assets determines solvency. Household liquidity (all assets except real estate, equities and private business ownership) was over 250% of household liabilities in 1952 and always exceeded liabilities until 1997 – but had fallen to 49% in 2007, one-fifth of its former level. However, the average tells us nothing about the distribution of those who can service their debts relative to those who cannot.

Owners' equity in their real estate holdings fell in the biggest real estate bull market in history because the rate of increase in debt exceeded that of prices. Owners' equity in their homes has fallen from over 80% in the 1950s to 43% at the end of 2008 – the lowest figure ever. Zillow.com reports that homeowners lost $6.1 trillion of market value from the peak in 2006 to the fourth quarter of 2008, at which time 17.6% of homeowners had negative equity in their homes. Foreclosures constituted one-fifth of all real-estate transactions in 2008 and all these figures are rapidly worsening as house prices fall. Credit problems normally result from economic slow-downs, but this time the credit problems started before the slowdown began.

The recession is aggravating the credit problems, as is sharply falling US household net worth. Harvard University's 2009 *State of the Nation's Housing* report showed 15.8% of all households and 47% of low income households are spending more than half their income on housing, so ever more households are falling into dire financial straits. Over 11% of all mortgages were either delinquent or in some form of foreclosure at the end of 2008. In addition, default rates on all types of consumer debt keep rising significantly from year-earlier levels quarter after quarter because most people have suffered falls in their living standards (see Figure 2.1 on page 41).

Real income growth in the US has been slowing, especially in the last decade or so, and the growth has been skewed towards females and the rich. Census bureau figures show males in full-time, year-round employment have had no rise in living standards in over 30 years. Their median income was $42,261 in 2006, less than in 1972 when it was $42,970 measured in 2006 dollars. Median female income calculated in the same way grew from $24,863 to $32,515. Median income fell from 86% of the average to 72% over the same period, so income growth for the rich outpaced income growth for females. Real income growth for all but the most highly paid workers ended in 1999. Internal Revenue Service figures show that the average real income per taxpayer fell between 2000 and 2005, and tax cuts did little for the average family as 62% went to the 0.25% of tax payers who earn over $1 million a year.

With real incomes slumping, the consumption binge could continue into this century only through consumers using their homes as ATMs. Falling interest rates and rising house prices let consumers increase the mortgages on their homes and withdraw the difference without raising the monthly payments too much. 'The strong pace of MEW [mortgage equity withdrawal] may have boosted annual consumption growth by 1 to 3 percentage points in the first half of the present decade.'[20] Lack of MEW means average GDP growth in borrow-and-spend nations will remain below previous trend growth rates until household saving and balance sheets have been restored to normality.

Falling food prices and interest rates have taken the sting out of the weak income growth in recent economic cycles. The part of the average household budget spent on food plummeted in developed nations (by over half in the US) over the past few decades, boosting non-food consumption beyond the growth in real incomes. This palliative is no longer available as food prices have reversed and will be on an upward trend for the foreseeable future. Energy prices have been rising too, and political concerns such as carbon footprints and renewable energy mean that energy prices will rise far higher than necessary. Also, because the population is ageing, retirement will reduce incomes for a growing number of people at the same as their medical costs are rising.

Rising food, energy and medical costs have ignited fears of inflation similar to those in the 1970s. However, at that time inflation was caused by central banks increasing the money supply to ease the shocks from big rises in energy costs in an economy that had excess demand most of the time. The competition for labour quickly diffused the higher prices into incomes, which then increased demand, which then increased prices and so on in an upward spiral.

The 21st century differs from the 1970s. Average output growth has been below trend in most developed nations this century and will slow further. Even services are now tradable and the substitution of Asian for North American and European labour has resulted in declining real incomes for many workers in America and Europe. Also, as will be discussed later, a deflationary credit contraction will occur in spite of government efforts to prevent it. Diffusing price shocks into income will be hard, so rising food and energy prices are more likely to contract demand (as do tax hikes), especially if the rising prices cause an inflation scare and rising interest rates.

The rising interest rates in the 1970s caused a banking crisis in the 1980s. A robust economy, high saving and strong balance sheets meant interest rates had to rise a long way to reverse rising inflation. It is different today. A weak economy, low saving, trashed balance sheets and falling living standards for many mean a much smaller rise in interest rates will reverse rising inflation this time. Interest rates fell to 40-year lows in 2003, more than offsetting the rise in household debt since the early 1980s. However, household debt service costs have risen slightly above the highs of the 1980s since 2003 (see Figure 3.5). Worse, the Fed's financial obligations ratio is now 19% compared with a high of 17% in the 1980s.

The rapidly escalating default rates and poor income outlook have reduced households, the backbone of the economy, to a spent economic force. Business and government combined make up less than one-third of the economy and both depend on households for their revenues, except for infrastructure investment. The American

Figure 3.5 **US household interest costs, 1946–2008**

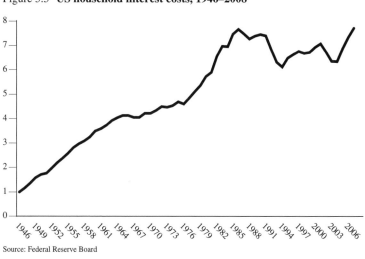

Source: Federal Reserve Board

Society of Civil Engineers' 2005 *Report Card for America's Infra-structure* gave the US a D grade and estimated an additional investment of 3% of GDP per year for five years would be needed to bring the infrastructure up to a reasonable standard. The report gathers dust with so many others, and infrastructure investment has remained about 1% of GDP. Housing is in an even sorrier state.

The latest housing slump has been far sharper than the previous one, which began in 1989. The ability to service mortgage debt has fallen as mortgage debt in the fourth quarter of 2008 was 57% of the market value of residential real estate, well above 1989's 35%. Few first-time home buyers put any money down in the final couple of years of the housing boom and tighter mortgage lending standards are limiting their refinancing options as mortgage rates fall. Also, speculators accounted for a big proportion of house sales during the boom. Most of them are suffering negative cash flows and so are trying to sell or are forfeiting their deposits, adding to the glut of homes for sale from defaults and repossessions. The poor state of the housing market has caused significant financial problems.

Delinquencies on consumer debt doubled in 2008 and the delinquency rate on all mortgages rose to a post-war high of 8% at the end of 2008. An additional 3% of all mortgages were in some stage of foreclosure, putting 11% of residential mortgages in trouble.[21] Moreover, First American CoreLogic reported mortgages with negative equity had risen to 8.3 million, 20% of the total.[22] The irresponsible lending in 2006 and early 2007 make further rises inevitable. About 62% of banks' earning assets are mortgage related, up from 38% in 1989. Also, banks booked the market rate of interest on negative-equity mortgages as income – not the amount received – so their income was overstated, aggravating losses as mortgage defaults rose. As a result, the viability of the entire banking system has come into question.

The big overinvestment in housing ended the credit cycle and the private sectors in borrow-and-spend nations must repair their balance sheets, so private-sector credit will contract.

Credit contraction is a strong deflationary force

Credit contractions caused depressions every 20 years or so from the Industrial Revolution until the Second World War, but more than 60 years have elapsed since the last one. Many people see this as a triumph of modern economic management but, as highlighted in the introduction, it was not. Underlying conditions strongly supported protracted prosperity after the war. High investment in plant and equipment created rising living standards for everyone until inflation soared in the 1970s and caused a credit crunch at the end of the decade.

Then, rising competition from emerging nations made investment in plant and equipment in developed nations a high-risk strategy. Restrictions on inward investment in emerging nations, the

84

obvious place for such investment after the credit crunch, further reduced investment in physical facilities. At the same time, financial innovation greatly increased liquidity, which, with plummeting inflation, reduced interest rates and made investment in financial assets extremely attractive.

Vast sums chasing a limited supply of financial assets (the high leverage in housing makes it a financial asset) pushed their prices to record highs and their yields to record lows. Desire for higher yields encouraged investors to seek ever more credit risk and to keep gearing up their balance sheets. This was sustainable as long as interest rates were either lower than inflation rates or falling as fast as debt was rising. However, ever higher debt ratios guaranteed rising defaults and, ultimately, a banking crisis.

Defaults usually start to rise after growth has fallen and profits have peaked. However, defaults began to rise before growth fell or profits peaked in 2008, a sure sign that the banking crisis that started in 2007 would be worse than most. The World Bank published a paper entitled *Managing the Real and Fiscal Costs of Banking Crises* in 2002. It studied 30 years of banking crises in 94 countries and showed governments had spent an average of nearly 13% of GDP on:

- open-ended liquidity support;
- blanket deposit guarantees;
- regulatory forbearance;
- repeated recapitalisations;
- debtor bailout schemes.

Each of these measures greatly increased the costs of banking crises. If the countries had not pursued any such policies, costs would have averaged about 1% of GDP, not 13%. Also, the authors saw no indication of these higher costs reducing the scale of the output dips that followed the crises. These damning findings certainly apply to emerging nations, which suffered some colossal losses from banking crises, such as the estimated 55% of GDP loss from trend incurred in the collapse of Argentina's currency board in 2001. However, they also apply to developed nations, for example the savings and loan collapse in the US in the 1980s and 1990s and the 1996 rescue of Japan's zombie banks, which cost more than $100 billion in public funds and two years later another $500 billion – some 12% of Japan's GDP.

In fact, the average loss in emerging nations was only slightly bigger than the average loss in developed nations. The important point is that the oft-repeated claim that bailouts help everyone is not true, and economically the best thing governments can do in banking crises is nothing. Even so, all the schemes criticised by the World Bank are being used again – so the outcome will be far more expensive than it need be. Also, the added government debt will increase interest costs far into the future. Increasing interest costs will raise taxes and lower living standards.

The diminishing amplitude of business cycles up to 2008 convinced most people that the worst possible event would be a minor and temporary slowing in growth. Such unbridled complacency occurs only at the major financial peaks that have occurred every 100 years or so, that is, the 1720s, 1830s and 1920s. We know we are at another such peak because this credit cycle ended when underlying conditions in industrial nations had become as negative as they had been positive after the war. Baby boomers were retiring and birth rates dropping. Negative demographics and economic leadership gravitating to emerging nations raised competition in markets that were growing ever more slowly. Consumers in industrial nations were hobbled by massive debts, rising energy and food prices, and the rising costs and diminishing benefits of retirement plans.

Business and governments were also in poor condition to withstand adversity. Many companies had reduced their credit ratings from investment grade to junk. Others had raised their political and business cycle risks by moving operations to fast-growing emerging nations, while geopolitical tensions were threatening both physical security and the flow of supplies. Most governments had begun to renege on commitments to their citizens – pensioners, for example. Euro-zone governments had raised their risk of default by issuing debt in a currency they cannot print. As a result, the credit crunch has begun credit liquidation in the private sector.

From credit crunch to credit liquidation

Sellers for future delivery originally had to deliver the contracted amount of the stated item to their buyers on the contracted date, limiting the total amounts of the contracts for future sale to amounts that could be delivered. Now cash payments settle most derivatives, allowing the total amount of derivatives to exceed the total amount of their underlying items by many times. The unintended consequence of this change is that derivatives often dominate their respective cash markets. Chapter 1 showed how oil futures determined the price of oil on world markets and Chapter 6 will show that rules for commodity futures must be changed to protect cash markets.

The credit crunch rendered exotic debt markets dysfunctional. The amount of US asset-backed commercial paper outstanding at the end of 2008 was down almost half from its high, and Canadian non-bank sponsored asset-backed commercial paper remained completely frozen for well over a year. The stock prices and credit ratings of monoline insurers (that is, insurers that had insured only state and local debt) plummeted because they had insured a lot of levered structured finance debt, such as CDO. CDO issuance in 2008 was down 88% compared with 2007. Participants are hoping for a revival, but their hope will be frustrated. Auction rate securities are slowly being unfrozen following the successive failures of auctions in 2008 (which prevented holders of the debt from liquidating their holdings), but future auctions are unlikely. State and local bonds are reeling as a result of the problems of monoline insurers and the seized-up auction rate markets. After-tax yields on AAA-rated state and local bonds rose to more than double the yields of similar term Treasury yields.

However, counterparty risk created the biggest fear in financial markets. Counterparty risk is the risk that the party on the other side of the contract will not fulfil its obligations. No provisions are made for counterparty losses or reserves held, so in the interdependent, highly levered, modern financial markets one default could start a string. Bear Stearns was one of only five big investment banks that were counterparties to 95% of over-the-counter derivative contracts. A run on Bear Stearns in March 2008 induced the Fed to bail it out for fear that its bankruptcy would have posed systemic risk from counterparty losses.

The Fed put $29 billion of dodgy Bear Stearns collateral into an off balance sheet vehicle as part of the bailout (after having insisted on Treasury securities as collateral for loans to the banking system for decades), loosened its collateral requirements and extended its lending facilities to investment banks. As well as more loans with easier terms, the Fed exchanged over $300 billion of Treasury securities for dodgy debt on investment banks' books in an effort to clear dysfunctional markets. However, true to the World Bank's *Managing the Real and Fiscal Costs of Banking Crises,* the bailout solved nothing. Credit problems worsened, the Treasury reorganised the mortgage giants Fannie Mae and Freddie Mac, and market confidence in banks' stocks evaporated.

The Philadelphia stock exchange bank stock index fell from almost 7% of the S&P 500 to under 4% between February and August 2008. As a result, the Lehman Brothers bankruptcy put the we-must-do-something contingent into high gear and they bailed AIG out a day later. A rapid succession of liquidity-enhancing schemes, bailout packages and fiscal stimulation measures followed. Credit conditions began to ease in October, but the Philadelphia bank stock index continued on down to less than 3% of the S&P 500 in February 2009. Both the commercial and the shadow banking systems face the worst solvency problems since the Great Depression, and the US consumer price index (CPI) falling below year-earlier levels has made some people believe the problems are even worse now.

Deflation under fiat money

Most people had believed fiat money made deflation impossible – because there would always be ways to inflate the money supply – before Japan's long deflation. The Fed still believes that shifting enough private debt onto the government's balance sheet – that is, socialising private losses – will prevent deflation. Japan's experience suggests this is not so: deflation has persisted for almost two decades despite the national debt ballooning to over 170% of GDP. The enormous expansion of the government balance sheet prevented the drastic drop in money supply and the resulting downward spirals of prices and output that occurred in the 1930s. However, as the World Bank pointed out, the economic and social costs probably would have been less if the government had done nothing.

The US has fallen into the same trap, and so the adjustment process will be prolonged. The end of the credit cycle is deflationary. Governments are spending $15 trillion or more in bailouts and fiscal stimulation, but the Asian Development Bank estimated the loss of wealth to the end of 2008 at $50 trillion, not only three times as much but also a huge proportion of global net worth, perhaps as much as 50%. Some 15 years of private debt liquidation followed the excessive growth in debt in Japan in the 1980s and the same will probably occur in developed nations, regardless of the size of the quantitative easing.

Quantitative easing more than doubled the size of Japan's monetary base in the three years 2001–03 (see Figure 3.6). Its

89

Figure 3.6 **Japanese monetary base, 1998–2009 (in 100 million yen)**

Source: Bank of Japan

Figure 3.7 **Japanese M2, 1998–2009 (in 100 million yen)**

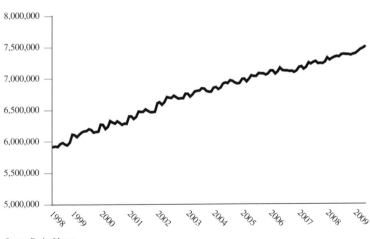

Source: Bank of Japan

level measured in dollars was higher than America's, even though Japan's economy was little more than one-third the size of the US economy. It reduced interest rates to minuscule levels, but that did little to promote growth in Japan. Instead, it encouraged foreigners to borrow yen to fund purchases of higher yielding assets in other currencies and so distributed Japan's excess liquidity throughout the world. Japan's money supply kept growing (see Figure 3.7), but that did not prevent deflation because money velocity fell.

Money velocity is the number of times each unit of money is used in a year. The inverse of money velocity is the Marshallian K, which shows the proportion of GDP the public wants to hold in liquid resources. Money with zero maturity (MZM) measures the stock of money that is available on demand from both commercial banks and shadow banks (see Figure 3.8). Public desire for liquidity halved from almost 60% of GDP to a little under 30% during the Great Inflation because interest rates were lower than inflation rates, so cash balances kept losing purchasing power. Public desire for liquidity more than doubled to well above the previous high in the two decades after the credit crunch. First, interest rates were higher than inflation rates and cash balances kept gaining purchasing power, then the credit crunch instilled a high level of fear and a corresponding desire for high cash balances.

Liquidity is the antithesis of leverage. Rising leverage is expansive in the short run and inflationary in the long run. Rising liquidity is contractive in the short run and deflationary in the long run. Wall Street wants yet another debt-fuelled asset boom; Main Street wants more liquidity. Wall Street has the Treasury and the Fed on its side. That is not enough, however, because Main Street owns almost 70% of the nation's net worth, much of which came from asset prices being inflated by the credit bubble. Falling asset prices are now deflating household net worth. This will keep fuelling Main Street's desire for liquidity, as will risk-averse bankers tightening lending standards and rising levels of bankruptcy.

Figure 3.8 **Marshallian K – MZM, 1959–2009, as % of US GDP**

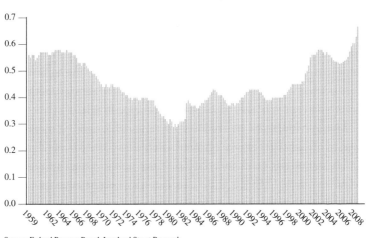

Source: Federal Reserve Board; Lombard Street Research

A rising desire for liquidity (or a falling desire to reduce liquidity) has reduced inflation in every slowdown for decades, and will keep doing so. The private sector in borrow-and-spend nations has run out of the ability to increase its debt levels, so inflation has fallen below target levels in many of them. In fact, current debt levels are unsustainable without either interest rates falling and lowering debt service costs or inflation rising and lowering the real debt load. Neither of these palliatives is likely.

First, sovereign interest rates fell to minimal levels in many nations in 2008, and the rise in 2009 is probably the first of many steps in a long-term rise. Second, private credit liquidation will keep downward pressure on growth and prices until the amount of debt outstanding falls to where creditors feel it is acceptably collateralised. Ballooning debt raised asset prices more than incomes and output prices, and private debt liquidation is hurting asset prices more than incomes and output prices. Optimally, incomes would remain stable and output prices would fall slowly.

A little inflation is not a good thing

Treating the value of the currency and full employment as separate problems arose from a theory, originated in the 1920s, that reducing inflation would increase unemployment and lowering unemployment would increase inflation, so monetary policy had to find the optimal trade-off between them. Belief in that trade-off created a widespread notion that a little inflation is a good thing, and its proponents use four main arguments to support their case:

- The effect of overall price stability is uneven. Manufacturing prices have been falling while services prices have been rising.
- A little inflation enhances growth.
- A little inflation facilitates the smooth operation of labour markets and so promotes maximum employment in the face of nominal wage rigidity.
- A little inflation keeps nominal interest rates from falling too close to the zero boundary, giving central banks enough room to cut rates should a recession appear imminent.

All four arguments are false. The first assumes that falling prices hurt manufacturers, so central banks should aim for a little inflation to prevent manufacturing prices from falling. However, monetary policy can change only the overall level of prices; it cannot change relative prices. Productivity gains are bigger in manufacturing than in services. Competition ensures that those productivity gains will keep reducing the prices of manufactured goods relative to the prices of services, regardless of what central banks do.

As to the second argument, inflation does not enhance growth; it impedes growth. From 1968 to 1983, US year-on-year inflation was never under 4% and average real GDP growth was well below potential at 2.5% a year. Inflation was over 4% in only eight months from 1991 to 2007, yet real GDP growth of 3.1% was close to potential growth. Inflation lowers growth because tax is levied on nominal interest and capital gains income. Martin Feldstein and others have shown that reducing inflation to zero would yield big and permanent real income gains, as inflation-related tax distortions significantly reduce real performance.[23]

Also, inflation makes it hard to distinguish relative price changes from movement in the aggregate price level. This ambiguity leads to errors in the assessment of prospective investment returns and so to the inefficient allocation of resources. Misallocation of resources lowers rates of real growth. Pessimistic price forecasts lead to under-investment and overoptimistic forecasts lead to defaulted debts and restrictive credit conditions. A credible monetary policy of stable inflation would remove uncertainty about future inflation. That stable rate need not be zero; it simply needs to be predictable. However, a steady positive inflation rate is harder to maintain than a steady zero rate because political pressure to lower rates to generate real economic gains is so much stronger than political pressure to raise rates to protect the purchasing power of the currency.

The third argument for a little inflation is that the rigidity in nominal wages would stop wages from adjusting to changes in the relative positions of particular firms, industries or occupations if inflation were zero. That is, inflation greases the wheels of labour market adjustment by letting some wages fall relative to other prices or other wages. This argument has three flaws. First, the price system allocates resources by setting relative prices so nominal wage rigidity would not survive in a zero-inflation regime. Jobs appear and disappear, and people move into and out of them so fast that the reallocation of labour dwarfs employment growth. Competitive forces eliminate anything that interferes with relative price adjustment that is not mandated by law or culture, so few labour markets in developed nations suffer from any big inefficiency.

Second, the grease-the-wheels argument assumes that only

cutting the nominal wage or letting all other prices around it rise can adjust mispriced wages, but two other mechanisms exist. Average real compensation rises as overall productivity rises, and real compensation tends to increase with seniority. Individual workers typically receive increasing real wages through time, so nominal wages may not need to fall with zero inflation, even in declining occupations. Advancing or delaying wage change relative to an individual's upward-sloping real wage path can accomplish the adjustments inflation enables.

Third, inflation puts more sand in the wheels than grease. A Cleveland Fed study[24] showed that managements decide on the overall size of their wage pools based in part on the expected rate of inflation, then adjust individual wages and salaries in accordance with those budget constraints. 'Sand' results from poor inflation forecasts in the first stage, causing suboptimal wage and salary increases. A firm may wish to attract high-quality applicants and fail to do so because the general level of wages rose faster than forecast. Also, workers' reactions to their pay rises often increase this sand effect by leading job seekers to incorrectly accept or reject offers because of confusion between real and nominal wages. The study estimated the grease and sand effects separately. The grease effect was statistically indistinguishable from zero, even for low inflation rates, while the sand effect rose rapidly with the inflation rate.

The fourth argument for a little inflation assumes a much more constant economic response to interest rate changes throughout the range of interest rates than actually exists. Figure 3.9 shows nominal three-month Treasury bill rates have generally followed the inflation component far more than real Treasury bills for the past 40 years. The nominal rate seldom followed the real component unless both the real and inflation components were moving in the same direction. The zero boundary view assumes coefficients derived from this history accurately estimate the effects of interest rate changes in the context of zero inflation, but they do not. The

Figure 3.9 **US three-month Treasury bills, headline inflation and real Treasury bills, 1959–2009**

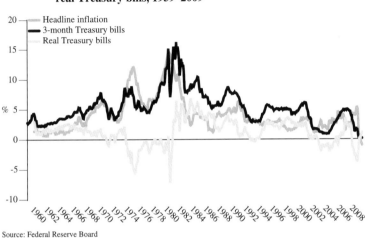

Source: Federal Reserve Board

relative stability in output growth, inflation and interest rates over the past two decades shows that low inflation produces a less variable economy.

The economy responds far more to changes in the real component of nominal interest rates than to changes in the inflation component, so the economic impact of a given interest rate change, measured in basis points, rises as interest rates fall. Thus if inflation goes to zero and is expected to remain there, the inflation component of interest rates falls to zero and the nominal rate becomes the real interest rate. The gold standard era shows the economic impacts of small basis point rate changes were enough to maintain high growth rates with no inflation, even deflation. For example, wholesale prices fell by about 2½% a year in Britain between 1870 and 1896 while output grew by 4% a year.

The classic gold standard made zero long-term inflation credible and, from 1843 to 1914, British long bond yields ranged from a peak of 3.6% (in 1848) to a low of 2.4% (in 1895). Only small variations in long-term interest rates kept the economy on a non-inflationary track because the gold standard's automatic stabilisers both allocated capital efficiently and limited credit creation, nipping both inflation and deflation in the bud. The Bank of England (BoE) maintained this stability by adjusting the bank rate to keep the ratio of its gold reserves to its outstanding notes in a range consistent with non-inflationary growth.

Gold yields nothing, so the public desire to hold it depended on the rate of return on other assets. Higher interest rates raised the opportunity cost of holding gold, so the public desire to hold it fell. Convertibility made sure the unwanted gold went into the BoE's reserves, raising its liquidity ratio to the desired level. Similarly, lower real interest rates increased public desire to hold gold and so drained the BoE's reserves to the desired level. This price stability did not eliminate business cycles, unemployment, or occasional financial distress – but it did minimise all three. Moreover, all three rose whenever nations went off the gold standard, so the optimum inflation target is 0%. Unfortunately, we do not know how to achieve 0% average inflation without the automatic stabilisers inherent in the classic gold standard. This problem will be examined in the next chapter.

Conclusion

The underlying conditions in industrial nations have gradually changed from very positive for growth at the end of the Second World War to very negative now. Simultaneously, rising debt gradually eroded balance sheets from very strong to very weak. Much of the added debt was used to buy existing assets, driving their prices higher. Lending became ever more irresponsible until most borrowers could no longer pay the interest on their debts from income.

Lenders depended on ever rising asset prices for their security. Ultimately, when even extremely irresponsible lending could not bring in enough borrowers to keep house prices rising, the credit bubble burst and the third stage of the credit cycle ended.

Strategic Economic Decisions, an economic advisory firm, estimates that household net worth in the US has averaged about 3.4 times GDP since 1950. The serial asset booms in the 1980s and 1990s raised it to about 4½ times just before the dotcom bust, but it has since fallen to 3.6 times GDP. Household net worth peaked in Q2 2007, and Fed figures show that it fell $13 trillion in the following six quarters. This fall, an annual rate of 14%, is unprecedented since the Great Depression and will probably take household net worth well below the average ratio of GDP before it recovers.

Trashed private-sector balance sheets constitute a formidable adversary to the Washington–Wall Street Axis desire to inflate forever. Inflation limits the benefits of growth to a small group and is counterproductive because optimal rates of growth in output and living standards have been sustained better in periods of deflation. Inflation misallocates resources because entrepreneurs mistake the liquidity central banks inject for real saving and so overestimate their potential markets – the major cause of business cycles.

The pain caused by adjusting from the narrowly based, US-centric growth fuelled by debt to widespread growth fuelled by saving is both real and unwelcome. Governments are desperately trying to inflate as a result, but the bursting of the credit bubble has made the liquidation of private-sector debt inevitable. Morgan Stanley estimates that the 15 largest banks shrank their balance sheets by $3.6 trillion up to the end of 2008 and will shrink them another $2 trillion in 2009. Slow growth and the pressing need to repair private-sector balance sheets makes deflation much more likely than inflation in most nations.

Creating the conditions needed for another sustainable credit expansion will take a long time. The financial industry and government were the big winners from inflation and should be the big losers in the next decade or two. Furthermore, the global monetary system should undergo significant reform.

4

The global financial system: not fit for purpose

The automatic stabilisers inherent in the gold standard continue to anchor financial thinking almost 100 years after the classic gold standard and the automatic stabilisers it built into the monetary system ceased to exist. The classic gold standard mandated gold and currency be interchangeable at a fixed and constant rate and bank reserves be held in gold. Bank reserve ratios were also fixed, so a given flow of gold into banks from private hands or international transactions would raise bank reserves and the money supply by a known amount. Similarly, a given outflow of gold would lower bank reserves and the money supply by a known amount. Currency convertibility and the need to settle international balances in gold meant nations with current account deficits in excess of capital inflows automatically experienced deflationary gold outflows. The loss of gold triggered a rise in short-term rates and a fall in prices until the outflow stopped. This prevented governments from pursuing inflationary policies. The rising short-term rates raised the opportunity cost of holding gold, so bank reserves rose as investors converted gold into interest-bearing paper. Similarly, a gold inflow raised bank reserves, triggering a drop in interest rates and a rise in prices. Falling short-term rates reduced the opportunity cost of holding gold and bank reserves fell as investors converted interest-bearing paper into gold until the inflow was sterilised and interest rates stopped falling.

Gold flows automatically altered short-term interest rates, so they changed frequently. The Bank of England changed the bank rate as many as 24 times in a year, although the odd year passed by with no change. Small interest rate changes would often stem gold flows, even reverse them. However, reserves were small and flows had to be stopped quickly, so sometimes big changes were needed. The close association between bank reserves and short-term rates not only stabilised output and prices in each nation on the gold standard, they stabilised financial markets too.

The current theory that financial markets tend towards equilibrium was true under the classic gold standard because the monetary stabilisers inherent in the system made departures from trend short and quickly corrected. The monetary stabilisers made international capital flows a stabilising force without any need for international co-operation. Unfortunately, the classic gold standard ended in Europe in 1914 and automatic monetary stabilisers vanished with it.

The Genoa conference in 1922 replaced the classic gold standard with the gold exchange standard. It made the dollar the only truly convertible currency in order to validate British inflation. Other currencies were not convertible into gold coins, only into large bars suitable for international transactions, so ordinary citizens could not exchange notes and securities for gold and vice versa. Furthermore, Britain could redeem sterling with dollars instead of gold, and other countries could redeem their currencies with sterling. This system did not restrict British balance of payments deficits and inflation because other countries did not redeem their pounds for gold. They kept the sterling as bank reserves and inflated their domestic money supplies accordingly.

Britain induced the US to accumulate sterling to minimise the UK's loss of dollars and gold. Using foreign exchange reserves as the monetary base unleashed an inflationary boom in Britain and

Europe, so gold flowed into the US. However, America hoarded the gold instead of following the classic gold standard and putting it in bank reserves and permitting inflation. Ever more gold flowed into nations that did not join the inflation bandwagon, mainly the US and France. Worse, sterling balances soared far beyond Britain's ability to redeem them. France tried to convert its sterling balances into gold in 1931, but it was too late.

Britain could not comply and the gold exchange standard collapsed. The collapse of the international payments system caused runs on banks in all nations that had been on the gold exchange standard. The bank runs turned the severe recession caused by the stock market crashes and the Smoot-Hawley tariffs into the Great Depression. Governments and central bankers defend their desire for inflation by blaming the gold standard for the Great Depression. Unfortunately, this defence has come closer to fooling all the people all the time than any other prevarication known to mankind. This first attempt to create international fiat money turned a relatively severe recession into the Great Depression. The fallout from the second attempt, the Bretton Woods Agreement, may yet ultimately lead to the second Great Depression.

The Bretton Woods Agreement tried to repair the flaws in the gold exchange standard by denying sterling reserve currency status. However, differing inflation rates as a result of differing monetary polices became automatic destabilisers that guaranteed recurring financial crises would ultimately end the inflexible fixed exchange rate system. This happened when President Nixon shut the gold window in 1971. Shutting the gold window ended the sham that the world remained on the gold standard almost 50 years after the Genoa Conference had neutered the classic gold standard. The jumble of fixed and floating currencies that evolved thereafter is a mêlée rather than a system and its inherent confusion has greatly increased the incidence of banking crises.

Every major banking crisis has sparked efforts to design a better system, but a lack of international co-operation has thwarted every one. In addition, the Eurasian savings glut (see Chapter 2) created unsustainable imbalances of saving, and investment and international capital flows are creating big problems for many nations, especially small ones.

Rates of return determine the direction of capital flows. Under the gold standard, gold outflows automatically raised interest rates in nations with current account deficits, attracting the capital needed to fund the deficits and expand production. Now central banks do not raise interest rates until the economy is booming. The resulting capital inflows only add fuel to the fire. Similarly, gold inflows lowered rates and stimulated capital outflows in current account surplus nations. Now central banks lower rates to stimulate weak economies and that causes capital outflows that aggravate the weakness.

Furthermore, international capital flows are now so big that these pro-cyclical capital flows, adding existing cyclical drivers, overwhelm the monetary policies of small countries and create needless banking crises in nations with good credit ratings, such as in Norway in 1987, in Sweden in 1991, and in Hong Kong in 1997. This disruption forces overly defensive monetary and fiscal policies and excessive currency volatility onto nations that are doing nothing wrong. As a result, some are restricting flows of portfolio capital into and out of the country, and others have given up their independent monetary policies and either pegged their currencies to a major currency, usually the dollar or the euro, or adopted a foreign currency as their own.

Fiat money allows unlimited credit and leverage

In short, abandoning the gold standard rendered the international exchange rate mechanisms unfit for purpose. This has left financial markets rudderless and the unlimited credit available under fiat money has extended the timescale of cycles so far that mean reversion has become meaningless. The interest rate cycle that began from the low in yields in the late 1940s may have finally reached the next low in 2008, or that low may not occur for another ten years or more. Worse, credit outstanding relative to GDP (leverage) has risen continuously since 1940.

Unlike the classic gold standard, fiat money allows unlimited leverage, which has ended any tendency to equilibrium or reversion to mean in financial markets. Regulated institutions must meet capital requirements, but not all financial companies are regulated and capital requirements are easily avoided, so leverage under fiat money is unlimited. Leverage would be beneficial if it improved efficiency. However, it is harmful because it reduces efficiency. Companies cannot produce greater returns on total capital by gearing up because the gearing does not change total return. Leverage affects only the distribution of the return to different classes of capital. Highly levered companies run into far more financial difficulties than those with less leverage. Leverage generates more pain but not more gain, and so reduces the efficiency of financial markets.

Classic investment theory relies on investors analysing various securities and buying the ones yielding the best returns, given their tolerance for risk. If everyone did this all the time, markets would tend towards equilibrium as the theory predicts. Unfortunately, the theory is valid only if investors derive their expectations rationally and they have access to a broad range of independent analyses. Neither of these conditions holds true all the time.

Moreover, theory ignores the emotional input to investment decisions. Investment involves estimating future returns, which are uncertain. That uncertainty triggers hopes and fears. Rational analysis quantifies and justifies our expectations of rates of return, but our emotions – that is, the tension between our hopes and fears – govern the actual investment decisions. Born optimists have a bullish bias, born pessimists have a bearish bias and the rest of us swing between the bullish and bearish camps. Markets behave rationally if the swing group is relatively evenly divided between bulls and bears and ever more emotionally as the swing group shifts into the bullish or bearish camp.

Emotions always trump reason and the more emotions take over, the more markets react to changes in group psychology rather than to changes in 'fundamentals'. The 1630s, 1710s, 1830s, 1920s and 1990s featured the most egregious examples of emotional market booms. None of the countries involved was on the classic gold standard at the time. Its limitation on credit growth would have prevented the creation of enough credit to feed such big speculative bubbles.

No monetary system embodies the same limitations on credit creation as the classic gold standard, and the modern universal fiat money system is especially liberal. Not only was the time span between the last two spectacular bubbles the shortest, but also the recent bubble was arguably twice as extreme as the 1929 bubble. The price/earnings multiple on the S&P 500 was almost twice the 1929 peak in 2000 and the dividend yield was only about one-third of the 1929 dividend yield.[25] Such extreme valuations could be attained only through the increased leverage obtained from credit growing far faster than output.

Credit risk, market risk and liquidity risk

Investors face three risks in financial markets:

- credit risk – the risk debtors will not fulfil their obligations;
- market risk – the risk prices will move adversely; and
- liquidity risk – the risk of inability to trade securities in the amounts desired without significant adverse movement in market prices.

Credit risk is exogenous, that is, the factors that create credit risk exist outside the market itself. Market risk is mostly exogenous as many factors moving market prices, such as fiscal policy, monetary policy, current account balances, earnings, and so on, are determined by agents external to the market who must take into account many factors other than the market. The efficient markets hypothesis, the theory underlying all financial pricing and risk models, assumes that investors analyse credit risk and market risk rationally, estimate probabilities and invest accordingly. It is reasonably accurate when credit and market risks incorporate most of the ongoing risks and so markets behave fairly rationally.

Liquidity risk is small in rational markets and so is represented, if at all, by a small spread for market-making in computer models. Liquidity risk differs from credit and market risks because it resides totally in the market itself and so cannot be modelled in the same way as exogenous risks. The reaction of the players in the market to a proposed trade determines the liquidity of that security at that time. This reaction depends on market conditions at that time and is fairly predictable when conditions are within the range of normal experience for the time. This predictability makes liquidity risk low much of the time. However, when market conditions move outside the range of normal experience predictability disappears and liquidity risk soars.

An external shock can multiply liquidity risk in the short term. However, markets adjust quickly and liquidity returns to normal unless the shock affects markets in a fundamental way. For example, the start of the First World War and suspension of convertibility in 1914 raised liquidity risk in European bond and money markets for a long time. But not all shocks materialise quickly. Leverage has been increasing liquidity risk for decades and recent estimates are that liquidity now accounts for about 70% of the variation in asset prices.

The catastrophic losses from the 2007–08 credit crunch, now estimated to be $2.7 trillion in the banking system alone, are a result of the vaunted value-at-risk computer models virtually ignoring 70% of the risks they are supposed to be measuring.

Rising leverage let market players, especially hedge funds and investment banks, acquire trading positions big enough to distort markets with little capital. For example, a search for yield, rising asset prices, narrowing credit spreads and few defaults from 2002 to 2004 made many more people want to sell credit insurance than buy it, so premiums fell sharply, creating the opportunity for credit arbitrage. In late 2004 investors with high credit ratings could raise money at about 2% a year, buy BBB-rated corporate debt to yield about 6% a year, and offload the risk of default at a cost of about 1% a year by buying credit default swaps (CDS) from sellers of credit insurance. Such trades then virtually guaranteed profits of up to 3% a year.

Their popularity drove the spread between investors' cost of funds and yields on corporate bonds down to little more than the cost of credit insurance. In addition, insurance premiums were based on continuously rising asset prices and so were far too low to cover defaults when asset prices stopped rising. Corporate spreads plummeted by more than three-quarters (see Figure 4.1). Only a few of the 150 most frequently traded corporate names offered spreads wide enough to make more than minimal profits in such trades by late 2006. The sub-prime mortgage fiasco raised the cost of insuring mortgage-based loans in early 2007 and panic soon spread throughout the financial system. The cost of insuring all debt soared and corporate debt spreads soared in unison. The derivative tail, CDS, was wagging the bond market dog.

Derivatives are highly levered and, until recently, required delivery in kind. Every long position opens an offsetting short position, so delivery in kind limited the total of derivatives outstanding to deliverable amounts. Most derivatives now allow cash settlement. This removed the limit to the total amount of derivatives outstanding and they are now overwhelming cash markets. Chapter 1 showed how

Figure 4.1 **Yield spread BBB corporate bonds – Treasury bills, 1988–2009**

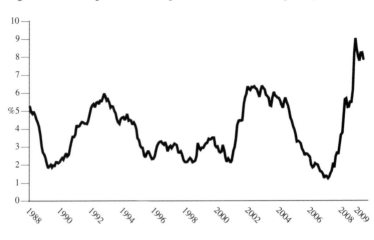

Source: Federal Reserve Board

investors controlled the prices of crude oil products by purchasing contracts for future delivery. CDS contracts did the same to bond prices. They do not require reserves for losses, collateral or margin, so can be infinitely levered. The $65 trillion or so of CDS contracts that were once outstanding insured about ten times the total reference debt. Their volume drove credit spreads down then up over the entire cash market.

The irresponsible lending resulting from structured finance and the much higher leverage resulting from derivatives have changed financial markets as much recently as the First World War and the end of the classic gold standard did almost a century ago. Structured finance greatly increased credit risk, and leverage has both greatly raised liquidity risk and enabled the aforementioned derivative tail to wag the bond market dog. Structured finance also embodied irresponsible lending because investors accepted asset-backed debt securities without the loan originators having to replace defaulted loans with good ones. Clearing markets of the bad loans resulting from structured finance will take years and financial markets will be under a cloud until most of the irresponsible loans have been purged.

Leverage creates the desire to trade more than markets can handle, so price rises and falls become steeper and extend further. Momentum analysis becomes far more profitable than basic analysis, so economic fundamentals affect financial markets ever less and momentum affects them ever more. Momentum players invade markets with vast sums looking for short-term gains without regard to or understanding of the primary economic forces. Momentum is pro-cyclical and leverage allowed momentum players to move markets pretty much as they pleased until the bubble burst.

These self-reinforcing rises and falls in prices from rising leverage multiplied liquidity risk. Ordinarily, this would not pose a problem. The poorer speculators would soon go broke, leverage would drop and markets would return to normal. However, asymmetric behaviour by the authorities now prevents this valuable market stabiliser from working. They do little to hinder asset prices from rising until the bubble bursts – and then not only do everything in their power to prevent asset prices from falling, but also bail out the unsuccessful speculators in order to perpetuate the bubble.

The asymmetric behaviour not only socialised losses and privatised profits, but also guaranteed debt loads would keep rising until the third stage of the credit bubble imploded. Governments still believe they can perpetuate the bubble by moving bad private debt onto public balance sheets. But moving debt from one balance sheet to another will not solve any problems, reduce the ultimate losses or prevent private-sector debt liquidation. Moreover, many market players, rating agencies, regulators and central banks remain unaware of the big changes needed to rectify financial markets. They are treating the current credit problems as temporary mark-to-market dislocations, but solvency (trashed private sector balance sheets) constitutes the real problem! Credit liquidation will be the eventual outcome and is the only solution.

The impact of the end of the credit cycle on asset prices

There is good credit and bad credit. Good credit transfers funds from savers to borrowers who can use that saving productively. Transferring saving never creates big economic problems. Lending printed money is bad credit. It increases the debt to GDP ratio, creating the three stages of the credit cycle explained in Chapter 3. The credit cycle enables us to live beyond our means by borrowing to advance future production and consumption into the present. The cycle ends when borrowers cannot service any more debt. Rapidly rising amounts of bad credit in the second and third stages of this credit cycle created the greatest series of asset bubbles of all time, so asset prices plunged when the bubbles burst. The dotcom and private equity busts trashed many corporate balance sheets and falling housing prices trashed household balance sheets.

Robert J. Shiller, professor of economics at Yale University, calculated an index of real prices for housing from 1890 to 2006. The index starts at 100 and for the first 110 years reached 125 only twice, in 1894 and 1989. That is, a house that cost $100,000 (in 2006 prices) reached $125,000 only twice up to 2000 and almost a century separated those peak readings. The price of that same house soared to $199,000 in 2006, double fair value. Real house prices were down by over one-third in early 2009, but they will have to fall further to reach fair value. The nominal price drop will be less, but that is scant comfort to homeowners facing such a sizeable drop in their net worth.

Stock markets face a similar situation. Profits rose to a record proportion of GDP in 2006 and remain far above normal. The financial industry contributed a large part of the increase in profits, and difficulties in that industry mean that the proportion of GDP going into profits will fall significantly. Like autos and pharmaceuticals in the past, the industry grew too big and government become involved. Government involvement gave the 'kiss of death' to profits in autos and pharmaceuticals and is doing the same to profits in financials.

Earnings grew at an average rate of only 4.5% a year for the 20 years ended in 2007, little over half the 60-year average of 8.4% a year. The fall in profitability in 2008 and the outlook for output growth and inflation give no indication that earnings will grow faster in the 20 years after 2007 than in the 20 before. Instead, the loss of outsized profits in the financial industry indicates a lower rate of growth, and dividend yields are well under average. Reinvested dividends has accounted for the lion's share of accumulated stock market returns, so the current multiyear lows in stock prices do not represent irresistible bargains.

The bubbles in commodities, art, memorabilia and so on that have occurred in the past couple of decades are equally unjustified. All these bubbles were products of the hugely extended credit cycle that the extremely lax supervision of fiat money has engendered. Chapter 3 explained the forecasting errors that inflation induces. These bubbles were the result of errors induced by 60 years of fiat money lowering lending standards and raising moral hazard by bailing out the undeserving.

A way forward

Restoring an efficient financial system requires overhauling the credit structure. Winston Churchill once said: 'You can always count on Americans to do the right thing – after they've tried everything else.' The only initiative from the myriad proposed so far that does not belong in the 'everything else' category is the effort to establish a market in covered bonds. On 28 July 2008 the US Treasury published *Best Practices for Residential Covered Bonds*, which should make them about as attractive to investors as insured deposits. The deposit insurance limit does not apply to covered bonds, widening their appeal.

A covered bond is backed by the cash flows from a pool of assets (usually mortgages) similar to mortgage-backed securities. However, the underlying assets remain on the bank's balance sheet and the bond is an uninsured debt of the bank. The bank must alter the composition of the asset pool to maintain its quality. It can also alter the terms of the mortgages, which avoids the current problem with mortgage-backed securities: who has the right to alter the terms of the underlying mortgages when borrowers get into trouble?

Best Practices calls for the bonds to be overcollateralised by 5% with high-quality mortgages with loan-to-value ratios of not more than 80%. Any loan that violated the loan-to-value ceiling, was more than 60 days non-performing or was delinquent would have to be replaced. This provision gives covered bonds a call not only on the bank's other mortgages, but also on its cash, Treasuries and agency securities, placing them ahead of other uninsured creditors. Covered bondholders also have a priority claim on the bank's entire revenue stream, not just the cash flows from the collateral, to meet required payments on the bonds.

Structured finance removed credit risk from the originating lender. Quantity of lending became far more profitable than quality, causing a disastrous collapse of lending standards. Leaving the credit risk with the originating lender makes covered bonds a superior business model. Banks are hoping covered bonds will give them a way of siphoning mortgage business away from Fannie Mae and Freddy Mac. This is a necessary move to return mortgage lending to the discipline of financial markets. Bank of America, JPMorgan Chase, Citibank and Wells Fargo believe the necessary legal, regulatory and market framework is in place to develop a covered bond market in America and will issue them. Substituting covered bonds for structured finance will increase financial market efficiency, but problems do exist:

- The prior claims of covered bonds will raise the cost of deposit insurance and put uninsured creditors, including taxpayers, at a disadvantage in defaults.
- Covered bonds are not familiar investments and look a lot like mortgage-backed bonds, whose unpopularity may limit demand.
- The FDIC will initially limit the outstanding amount of covered bonds a bank can issue to 4% of its total assets, limiting the supply too.
- The accounting treatment of such instruments is unclear, especially from a capital adequacy perspective.
- Covered bonds will be a source of long-term funding but will not have a broad, active market at first, so may be illiquid.

Covered bonds will not fulfil the US government's hopes for a quick fix to the nation's mortgage problems, but they will help limit irresponsible lending and leverage by leaving the assets on the books of the originating lender.

Conclusion

Markets cannot correct imbalances when governments keep assuming bad debts, as has occurred since the Penn Central bailout in 1970. The unlimited credit of fiat money has allowed ever more and ever bigger bailouts. Government 'solutions' for the problems of excessive debt all increase the amount of debt outstanding instead of correcting the excesses. Borrowing more to ease the problems created by too much debt has allowed the excesses to accumulate and pushed the day of reckoning into the future. The day of reckoning has now arrived, but governments are oblivious to it and are rushing off in all directions but the right one.

Leverage is most important variable needing regulation. The gold standard was the world's most successful monetary system because its monetary stabilisers limited leverage without the possibility of human intervention – which has been a dismal failure. For example, off-balance-sheet financing and leverage soared as capital regulations increased. Regulating leverage requires all liabilities to be recorded on balance sheets and all off-balance-sheet entities, such as special investment vehicles, to be banned. This would be relatively easy according to Michael Lewitt of Hegemony Capital Management, who wrote: 'Speaking as someone with extensive knowledge of these off-balance-sheet entities, it would not be difficult to render them extinct relatively easily. It would be doing the world a favour.'[26]

Balance sheets would also have to include the contingent liabilities embedded in derivative positions in order to assess leverage accurately. Derivatives held with the intention to deliver or receive in kind at the expiry of the contract should incur no more than a mark-to-market liability. All others should incur a contingent liability of the total value of the contract less the value of any assets or liabilities that are being directly hedged. In all cases, the liability should be reduced by any applicable margin, collateral and reserves. Precisely how this could be done is beyond the scope of this book.

Failing to regulate leverage created the perceived need for the consistent government bailouts that have created immense moral hazard in financial markets. The resulting irresponsible lending, structured finance and derivatives have turned financial markets into a giant pyramid scheme that is now collapsing. The next chapter will show that government efforts to get the private sector to borrow its way out of debt are doomed to failure.

5

We cannot borrow our way
out of debt

As we saw in Chapter 1, all the factors that had guaranteed good growth in developed nations for an extended period of time have turned negative in recent years, and relative price increases for food, water and energy will keep eroding the growth of real incomes over time. Chapter 2 added to the woes of the developing nations by showing that economic leadership is gravitating to emerging nations and a bloc may soon challenge US hegemony. Chapter 3 showed that a long, inflationary credit cycle has ended and deflation is probable. Chapter 4 explained why the financial system is not fit for purpose and should be radically overhauled. This chapter and the next will weave these different strands into assessments of financial institutions, the economy and markets.

It is clear that this is a period of significant change, so the future will differ greatly from the past. World growth will slow, probably by about half. Developed nations are likely to bear a disproportionate share of the decline, so the predicted big flow of immigrants from emerging to developed nations may not occur, even though the real rises in food and energy prices will affect emerging economies more than developed ones. Even if the predicted immigration does occur, growth in developed nations will not only lag behind growth in emerging nations, but also ultimately turn negative in the absence of continuing significant productivity growth. Later in this chapter, we will see why the required productivity growth is far from guaranteed.

Solvency, not liquidity, caused today's credit problems

US household net worth accounts for 70% of the nation's net worth and so is the foundation of the credit structure. Household net worth peaked in Q2 2007 and had fallen 21% ($13 trillion) by the end of the first quarter of 2009 – by far the biggest percentage decline in the history of the series. Equities accounted for about half the loss, real estate about 30% and losses in pension funds and other assets about 20%. Mortgage debt fell over 1% in the year to the first quarter of 2009, but house prices fell faster. Equity in household real estate fell from 59% in 2005 to 41%, a new record low. Falling household net worth created big problems in financial markets.

The TED spread (the three-month Eurodollar rate minus the three-month Treasury bill rate) is probably the most reliable indicator of immediate credit problems. In the absence of credit problems it ranges from about 10 basis points (bps) to about 60 bps. (A basis point is one-hundredth of 1%.) Spreads over 60 bps show financial problems are rising, especially in the present low interest rate environment, and spreads over 100 bps are a signal to reduce risk. The TED spread shot above 100 bps on 10 August 2007 and soared to a record high in October 2008 (see Figure 5.1). It has since fallen back but remains in the danger zone.

The Philadelphia bank stock index shows investors' perceptions of the health of banks. It began to fall sharply relative to the S&P 500 at about the same time as the TED spread began its meteoric rise but, unlike the TED spread, it has not yet approached previous levels (see Figure 5.2) because bank finances are deteriorating rapidly. The Texas ratio successfully identified banks likely to fail in the oil bust in Texas in the 1980s by comparing the ratio of banks' bad loans to

Figure 5.1 **TED spread, 1975–2009**

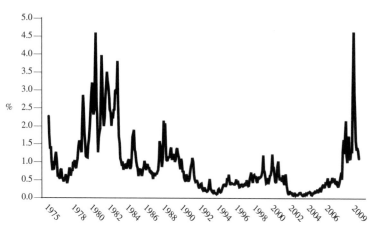

Source: Federal Reserve Board

their ability to absorb bad loans. Banks are likely to fail if the ratio exceeds 100%. The Texas ratio for the first quarter of 2009 for US commercial banks was 37.8%, more than three times the low in the second quarter of 2006 (see Figure 5.3). If the Texas ratio keeps rising as in the past, bank defaults will soar.

The Texas ratio is soaring because irresponsible lending and borrowing induced the collapse of the third stage of the credit cycle. Structured finance created vast amounts of bad debt and opaque securities of unknown value and raised leverage from almost non-existent to grotesquely excessive. The resulting collapse of structured finance (see Chapter 3) ended an expansion in leverage that had lasted for over 60 years and trashed both borrowers' and lenders' balance sheets. The collapse abruptly reduced liquidity from almost unlimited to almost non-existent and as a result lending standards quickly tightened.

Working our way back to 'normal' functioning of credit markets

Figure 5.2 **Philadelphia bank stock index – % S&P 500, March 2004–June 2009**

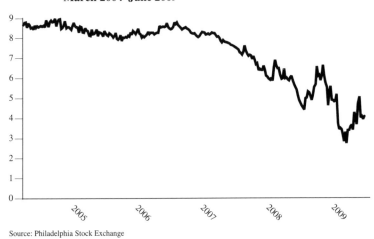

Source: Philadelphia Stock Exchange

Figure 5.3 **Texas ratio US commercial banks, Q4 2005–Q1 2009**

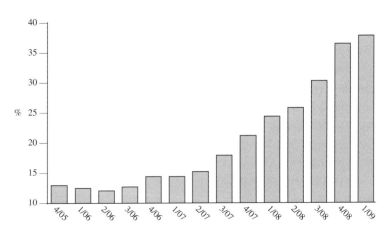

Source: Federal Deposit Insurance Corporation

will be a lengthy process and, as we will see later, governments are making it longer, more difficult and much more expensive than necessary. Off-balance-sheet vehicles to avoid capital regulations, severe downgrading of bank assets and mark-to-market losses have drained vast amounts of bank capital. The April 2009 IMF *Global Financial Stability Report* estimates that financial institutions will have to write off a total of $4.1 trillion of losses with $2.7 trillion accruing to banks. Banks had written off only $844 billion by the end of 2008 and so still have almost $2 trillion to write off. These estimates will probably be conservative, like all previous estimates.

Banks have recapitalised most of the losses they have written off, so we were more than a quarter of the way through the credit problems at the end of 2008. Governments have provided funds to recapitalise banks, against the World Bank's recommendations in *Managing the Real and Fiscal Costs of Banking Crises.* Rising defaults on mortgages, consumer debt and the opaque structured finance securities of unknown value remaining on bank balance sheets are the real problem. Some may be underpriced in today's turbulent credit markets, but others will end up having virtually no value.

The losses inherent in such securities must be identified and excised before banks can be capitalised properly and credit conditions can return to normal. Until then bank capital will be a financial black hole into which governments keep pouring money. Serial recapitalisations will decimate the equity of current shareholders in weak banks. However, governments and Wall Street do not want to know, so identifying toxic assets has a long way to go. Not only had the required private-sector deleverage barely begun by the end of 2008, but also a lot of the criticism of the banks was false.

Banks are not only lending, they are also investing

The considerable whining about banks refusing to lend notwithstanding, bank lending rose significantly all through 2008. In *Facts and Myths about the Financial Crisis of 2008,* the Federal Reserve Bank of Minneapolis showed four popular beliefs about the credit crisis that shaped fiscal and monetary policy were fiction, not fact:

*   Belief: bank lending to non-financial corporations and individuals declined sharply. Fact: bank lending rose throughout 2008 and some categories, such as commercial and industrial loans, rose sharply.
*   Belief: interbank lending was essentially non-existent. Fact: bank lending every week in October 2008 surpassed the former record highs for interbank lending established in July 2008. However, quantitative easing reduced the need for interbank lending thereafter.
*   Belief: commercial paper issuance by non-financial corporations has declined sharply. Fact: non-financial commercial paper outstanding rose to levels not seen since 2001.
*   Belief: banks play a large role in channelling funds from savers to borrowers. Fact: the Fed Z1 accounts show about 80% of non-financial corporate borrowing comes from non-bank sources.

These myths arose from extensive tightening of lending standards combined with a big drop in the ability of shadow banks to lend. Loose regulation and excessive leverage had allowed shadow banks to undercut commercial bank margins, but fear, losses and increased regulation sharply reduced shadow bank lending. US commercial banks, however, are lending freely to creditworthy borrowers. Debtors who should never have been granted loans in the first place are the ones that cannot borrow now. Higher costs in regulated banks and tightening lending standards together with falling loan demand have made most people think credit is tight.

The real problem is not bank lending, but the lack of creditworthy borrowers. However, that does not mean that banks are doing a good job. An IBM study found a big difference between what banks think their customers want and what customers actually want. Big banks remain wedded to the one-stop-shop model of banking, hoping for the return of the days of soaring profits from opaque products (such as over-the-counter derivatives) that allowed inefficient pricing. This intransigence may end the era of big banks.

IBM predicts that the best-performing banks will be much more specialist and more aligned with their customers' needs.[27] Specialist banks have seen their revenues grow 30% more than universal banks' revenues and enjoy operating margins of 25% compared with the 16% universal banks command. As a result, IBM sees the industry splitting into three segments:

- providing the infrastructure to facilitate capital allocation, relying on economies of scale to drive down costs;
- giving advice, such as wealth management firms and boutique M&A advisers;
- giving superior investment performance, such as private equity and hedge funds.

Differential profits may split the industry as IBM foresees, but bank regulation is high on the official agenda. Regulators may require some of the largest institutions to downsize or dispose of business lines, but that will neither turn banks into consumer-friendly operations nor increase bank lending.

Governments embarked on massive, but completely useless, bank bailout programmes 'to get banks lending again'. Their first intention was to increase liquidity, but short-term sovereign yields far below policy rates proved there was no liquidity problem. The risk-weighted capital requirement for sovereign bonds is zero, so banks used much of the bailout money to buy the debt that funded the bailouts. This drove sovereign yields far too low and did little to free up other financial markets.

The second intention was to raise capital adequacy. The US Treasury labelled its initial investment of more than $250 billion in US financial institutions 'a strategy to bolster the health of the banking system'. With the lack of creditworthy borrowers, however, banks used these funds to buy other banks. Bank of America used its $15 billion to double its stake in state-owned China Construction Bank – but is now in the process of selling the additional investment. PNC Financial Services Group used $5.2 billion of its $7.7 billion to help finance its buyout of National City. Removing smaller, weaker banks from the market may reduce the cost of defaults to taxpayers, but it also reduces the competition that benefited consumers by limiting the explosion in banking fees.

Continuing credit problems may make some of these expansions as counterproductive as the takeovers that humbled Citigroup, Bank of America and Royal Bank of Scotland (RBS). The US Treasury believes larger deposit bases can bear the weight of the bad assets better, but bank consolidation does nothing to identify or remove the billions of dollars of toxic assets that remain on banks' balance sheets. As a result, the programme merely gives big US banks a possible windfall tax gain of $140 billion through acquiring failed banks whose only real value is the losses on their books. The acquired banks' losses could offset the acquiring banks' gains and thus enable them to avoid taxes. Bank acquisitions helped accelerate worldwide deal-making in 2008 to a global volume exceeding $3 trillion.

Nevertheless, commercial banks offer a public good. This status gives them a public safety net, deposit insurance and access to a lender of last resort, in return for submitting to public regulation. The shadow banking system that financial innovation created after the credit crunch of the early 1980s operated just like the commercial banking system and its performance gave the public the confidence it was just as safe. This not only greatly increased the ability to fund illiquid assets, but also created the presumption that financial innovation could always fund highly levered positions in illiquid assets in shadow banks.

Soaring defaults from lending standards falling far below irreducible minimums invalidated that presumption. In addition, shadow banks lacked a public safety net, so were not as safe as commercial banks. Frozen credit markets rendered shadow banks unable to fund overlevered positions in illiquid assets, so the shadow banking system is unravelling, lending is being reintermediated and viable shadow banks are rushing to become regulated commercial banks. The increase in regulation guarantees the credit cycle has ended.

The end of every previous credit cycle resulted in credit being liquidated until lenders had confidence borrowers could service and repay their debts. The same should be happening now, but governments have succeeded in making credit grow faster than GDP by guaranteeing bank deposits and bank borrowing, taking bad loans onto their balance sheets and pumping money into banks through quantitative easing. As a result, the only sign of the necessary private-sector debt liquidation to the end of 2008 was a minor drop in US household debt in the fourth quarter. By contrast, government debt is soaring in borrow-and-spend nations. For example, US federal debt rose at a 44% annualised rate in the second half of 2008.

A paper presented to the American Economic Association by Carmen Reinhart and Kenneth Rogoff in January 2009 shows the average rise in government debt in the three years after a banking crisis is 86%, so many sovereign credits will be downgraded. Worse, some nations lack the resources needed to honour the liabilities they have assumed. Iceland has already reneged on its bank guarantees, and others will probably follow. At best, the higher interest costs will raise fiscal deficits significantly, impeding future saving and investment. This, in turn, will slow growth in GDP and living standards to minimal levels in borrow-and-spend nations for many years, if not decades.

Figure 5.4 **US real GDP growth, 1947–2009 (in US$ trillions)**

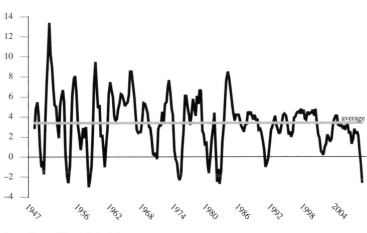

Source: Bureau of Economic Analysis

Growth has been much weaker than most people think

Growth in the 2002–07 recovery was weak (see Figure 5.4). Its peak barely exceeded the post-war average, even though the housing bubble and mortgage equity withdrawal greatly boosted consumption. People believed the economy was strong because rapidly rising house prices since the mid-1990s had created a 'feel good' factor that gave the illusion of much faster growth than was actually occurring. The US, and other economies, would have been in a long recession in this century without the artificial lift of rising asset prices, so a widespread recession was bound to occur soon after house prices stopped rising. The NBER dated the beginning of the recession to well before the credit crisis, so rising energy prices were the proximate cause of the global recession, but the end of the credit cycle increased its length and severity.

Continuing credit difficulties will add to the drag from ageing populations, competition from emerging nations and the loss of wealth, so low growth will persist in developed nations for a long time and cause significant problems. Chapter 1 showed investment is levered to growth and most developed nations are falling into the slow-growth category. Slow-growing economies need little investment and their productivity tends to fall, especially if the investment is not properly targeted.

Most people think of productivity as output per hour worked and take the productivity of capital as a given. If that were true, the high investment in the US in recent years would have created rapid growth. It did not because high tax rates together with ever increasing and more complex regulations inhibited entrepreneurship and strangled small and medium-sized enterprises, and government grants and subsidies favoured big multinational companies. Small and medium-sized enterprises develop far more inventions and technology than big companies. Favouring the big over the small caused declining innovation and productivity, which in turn misallocated capital to overinvestment in housing and political favourites.

This greatly reduced the productivity of capital (see Figure 5.5). Multifactor productivity is labour productivity plus capital productivity, and the falling trend of capital productivity has held multifactor productivity not only far below labour productivity, but also below the historical norm of about 2% a year. Falling capital productivity was the biggest factor causing the weak growth in the last two recoveries. Governments allocate capital badly. Big and rising government intervention in all aspects of the economy as well as private-sector deleverage will ensure poor capital productivity for the foreseeable future.

The credit bubble boosted asset prices far more than GDP growth; the credit bubble bursting is hurting asset prices far more than GDP growth. However, falling asset prices are creating a 'feel bad' factor that gives the illusion the economy is far worse than it really is. The recession is relatively severe, but the 2008 comparisons with the Great Depression were ridiculous.

Figure 5.5 **US capital productivity, 1987–2008**

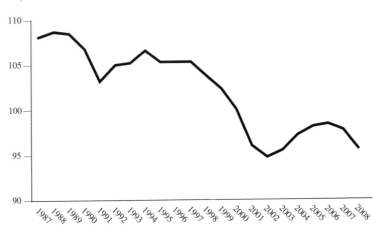

Source: Bureau of Labor Statistics

The end of the credit cycle is finally reversing the fall in savings rates in borrow-and-spend nations, but the economy is not imploding – and will not for three reasons:

- In 1931, the monetary system collapsed initiating the bank runs. The current monetary non-system is not fit for purpose, but there is no danger of it collapsing.
- In the 1930s, the public withdrawing gold from bank reserves caused severe drops in money supplies. That is impossible now because the public cannot withdraw bank reserves under fiat money. Central banks will make sure that money supplies do not fall.
- Protectionism is creeping in, but it is unlikely to match the retaliatory tariff war spawned by the Smoot-Hawley tariffs in 1930. Ending those tariffs initiated an immediate rise in global trade and output growth.

Bailouts do not work

The US had chronic fiscal surpluses in the 1920s. Treasury Secretary Andrew Mellon kept cutting taxes, but the surpluses kept growing because the transfer of money from the public to the private sector stimulated an investment and spending boom. Populist presidents Herbert Hoover and Franklin Roosevelt created massive spending programmes after the stock market crash, yet the US suffered more from the Great Depression than all major nations except France, which had its own version of the New Deal. US GDP per head fell from one-third more than Britain's in 1930 to equal Britain's in 1939.

More recently, Japan had nine fiscal stimulus packages costing a total of over $1.4 trillion at today's exchange rates in an economy less than one-third the size of the US economy. Japan's economy never gained sustainable growth, so they too failed. Today's fiscal policies are those same failed policies, but writ far larger, so they will fail even more spectacularly.

These policies trade short-term gains for long-term losses at best and just create losses at worst. Raising government deficits to provide fiscal stimulation can bring growth forward a bit, but financing the deficits either consumes saving or prints money. Governments opting for printed money since the Penn Central bailout in 1970 caused the second and third stages of the credit cycle that has now ended. In addition, governments pay down little of their debt and their borrowing is impervious to interest rates. The rising costs of servicing government debt perpetuate big deficits long into recoveries and so keep crowding out investment and lowering growth for decades.

Faith in free markets has never been robust – even in the US, the biggest backer of capitalism. Fear and expediency have created a consensus across the political spectrum that governments must spend whatever amount is necessary to stabilise housing markets, bail out financial firms, liquefy credit markets, create jobs and make the downturn as shallow and brief as possible. People want to see their governments acting to minimise their pain. The fact that their actions in the past have been useless at best and counterproductive at worst is immaterial.

This disregard for facts will be costly because markets run economies far better than governments. Excess credit causes banking crises and credit contraction is the only real antidote. The best thing governments can do is to let the automatic stabilisers built into the fiscal structure ease the pain. Unfortunately, fiat money gives governments unlimited scope for fiscal stimulation and substituting good government debt for bad private debt. They are doing massive amounts of both, even though *Managing the Real and Fiscal Costs of Banking Crises* found government intervention ineffective in reducing either the length or the severity of banking crises. That is because the intervention always raised structural deficits.

The same problem exists now as most governments ran big deficits in the 25-year boom since the credit crunch in the 1980s, largely in useless bailouts and fiscal stimulation. For example, *Corporate Welfare: Now a $182 Billion Addiction* by Canada's Fraser Institute argues that government subsidies to failing businesses (totalling about C$13,639 per taxpayer from 1995 to 2005) only delayed the inevitable. The bailouts also hurt healthy companies during times of economic stress because bailouts merely create zombie companies that take business away from productive companies in the same industry. The US is now turning two of the big three automakers into zombies with bailouts when Chapter 11 bankruptcy filings free of political interference would create a far stronger domestic industry.

Chapter 11 can rescue 'financially failed' companies, but it cannot rescue 'economically failed' companies. A typewriter manufacturer facing bankruptcy would be an economically failed company because the market for typewriters is small and shrinking. The company's financial, physical and human capital would be better redeployed elsewhere, such as making computers. A financially failed enterprise, however, is worth more as a continuing business than its break-up value. Chapter 11 exists to allow it to continue in business while reorganising.

The auto companies are financially failed enterprises because they need reorganisation but still make products consumers want. They have to renegotiate their labour and retirement contracts, modernise their distribution systems and probably replace management. Chapter 11 provides a chance to do all that with little inconvenience to consumers. Reorganisation would pare the weakest dealers while strengthening those that remain. Even so, the managements, the United Auto Workers Union (UAW) and the government insisted that 'bankruptcy is not an option' and 'would be the kiss of death' – because Chapter 11 would force them all to give something up.

The incumbent managers would probably become unemployed and Chapter 11 would place severe limitations on their compensation if they did not. A company can liquidate itself if the compulsory mediation process fails to reach an agreement, so Chapter 11 would force UAW workers to take pay cuts, revamp their cumbersome union work rules and reduce their gold-plated health and retirement benefits. The government interfered in Chapter 11 negotiations because it wants to use taxpayers' money to bribe automakers into manufacturing the cars favoured by 'green' politicians rather than the cars consumers want to buy. In short, a politics-free Chapter 11 would produce a much better outcome than any bargain struck by the incumbent management, the UAW and the government.

Bailing out householders is equally counterproductive. Credit Suisse raised its forecast that 6.5 million mortgages will be in foreclosure from 2009 to 2012 to 8.1 million, 16% of all US mortgages.[28] 'Despite some initial signs that sub-prime foreclosures were near a plateau, the combination of severe weakening in the economy, continued decline in home prices, steady increase in delinquencies, particularly in the prime mortgage space, ensure that foreclosure numbers, absent more dramatic intervention, will march steadily higher,' Credit Suisse wrote.

Credit Suisse's faith in intervention is misplaced. The Office of the Comptroller of the Currency tracked the number of borrowers that re-defaulted on their mortgages after they had been modified to make them 'affordable'.[29] After eight months, 58% of borrowers had re-defaulted and most of them will go into foreclosure. Further studies have increased that figure as high as 75%.

Even so, the Federal Deposit Insurance Corporation, supported by the House Financial Services Committee chairman, Barney Frank, wants to use an additional $24.4 billion of the $700 billion government bank bailout programme to modify more loans. The Office of Thrift Supervision claims that focusing on job creation is a better use of federal dollars. Regardless of who wins the argument, the residential mortgage situation is unlikely to get any better and a crisis in commercial real estate looms large.

Temporary tax cuts and rebates are equally counterproductive. Economics professors Milton Friedman and Franco Modigliani showed that consumers have a far greater tendency to spend permanent income than transitory income, so temporary tax cuts and rebates are mostly used to increase liquidity, as the US rebates were in 2008. The stimulative effect is especially low when the ratio of public debt to GDP is high. Swedish experience shows fiscal expansion may even result in contraction if consumers are worried about the fiscal sustainability of their governments. Fiscal stimulus was huge but counterproductive in Sweden's banking crisis in the early 1990s. The public debt grew so fast that people feared for the future of their nation and spent less. Moreover, risk premiums rose to the same level as in Italy, with its tradition of excessively loose fiscal policy.

Worse, the deficits stratify society. US Census Bureau figures show the real median earnings of full-time, year-round male workers fell at an average annual rate of 0.15% a year between 1973 and 2006, compared with a rise of 2.7% a year from 1960 to 1973 (1960 was the earliest year in this study). Clearly, a big change occurred in the early 1970s. That change was from fiscal budgets normally in surplus with only a few deficits to fiscal budgets normally in deficit with only a few surpluses. In addition, the average income for all households was 16% greater than the median income for all households in 1973, and 42% greater in 2006, so deficit financing makes the rich richer and the poor poorer.

Can emerging nations rescue developed nations?

Economic leadership gravitating to emerging nations has created an area of economic strength that may keep developed nations from falling into prolonged recession or depression. Low to negative growth in industrial nations is reducing their imports from the fast-growing emerging nations. Chapter 2 shows that domestic demand must rise sharply in emerging nations to keep world growth from slowing significantly. The stronger demographics in emerging nations together with domestic demand stimulation could soon return several emerging nations to trend growth. This would not only provide export markets to help developed nations out of their recessions, but also help reduce the huge saving and investment imbalances caused by the Eurasian savings glut.

Unfortunately, the requisite growth in emerging nation domestic demand is far from certain. The export share of GDP in developing Asia rose to a record high of 47% in 2008, up from 35% in 1997. China led the charge by raising exports from 20% of GDP in 2000 to 40% in 2008. Furthermore, rising food and energy prices have created bigger headwinds in emerging nations than in industrial nations and some emerging nations seem reluctant to move away from export-led growth. For example, China has announced big packages to stimulate domestic demand, yet also reversed the slow yuan revaluation to a slow devaluation and increased export rebates to bolster its flagging exports. Other emerging nations are giving similarly mixed messages.

Worse, the China miracle may be ending. The government has never been in total agreement about the wisdom or course of reform. In the early stages, economic reforms created many winners and few losers. Small-scale experiments often led to success on a national scale, such as allowing farmers to keep what they produced from private plots and the establishment of special economic zones along the coast. The major involvement of foreign enterprises in the Chinese economy was never planned. It simply evolved.

China became a remarkably laissez-faire economy in the late 1990s and early 2000s. The government's revenues as a share of GDP shrank to around 11%, from 31% in 1978, while it unilaterally cut tariffs and joined the World Trade Organisation. Inefficient state-owned enterprises shed about one-third of their workforce, about 60 million jobs, so China enjoyed almost double-digit trend growth for about three decades. Even so, there have been some notable failures, such as China's largely dysfunctional stock markets that cannot become a viable source of capital for entrepreneurs because that would hurt the state-owned enterprises and those who own their overpriced shares.

This lack of a true consensus on the virtues of free markets is shifting the communists-turned-capitalists back towards state control. The government raised national revenue back to 20% of GDP by improving the tax collection system. Government leaders now portray themselves as the answer to every problem – by using public resources to help those left behind by the new prosperity, rather than counting on new businesses to create jobs. China's social safety net is small compared with European nations, but it is expanding rapidly. China remains a poor country and has a rapidly ageing population, so increasing the social security safety net will be sustainable only if rapid growth continues.

Loss of exports as a result of the financial crisis and recessions in North America and Europe slowed China's growth sharply, perhaps into a brief outright contraction. At 40% of GDP, exports have been a major driver of the Chinese economy and export growth turned negative in early 2009. Import growth turned even more negative, so domestic demand probably fell too. Falling export and domestic demand growth together imply a harsh inventory cycle. The inventory liquidation should run its normal course over a couple of quarters and the end of the recessions in North America and Europe should return China to trend growth.

China's trend rate of growth going forward depends on its capital spending, which has been an unprecedented 40% of GDP. Rapid export growth validated the massive investment over the past few years, but deflation and rising private-sector saving in borrow-and-spend nations could limit China's export growth for a long time. Unfortunately, China seems to prefer to protect its exports with vicious price competition and currency devaluation than to stimulate domestic demand. Such defensive actions are likely to reduce China's trend growth.

American private-sector savings are rising, which will reduce the need to run current account deficits to import saving as long as the US funds its huge federal deficits by quantitative easing. The US economy is about five times the size of the Chinese economy in dollar terms and almost half of US imports come from China. If the rise in US saving cuts imports by 4% of GDP (to 2004 levels), China's domestic demand would have to grow by $5 \times 2\% = 10\%$ to replace the lost export sales to the US. Investment, consumption and government spending would have to replace those lost exports.

Chinese industry has never been particularly profitable. The reduction in volumes has created a severe margin squeeze, which has bankrupted many companies, greatly reduced inflows of foreign direct investment and removed any chance of self-finance to help sustain China's high level of fixed investment. The government will throw unlimited amounts of credit at loss-making enterprises to sustain investment at 40% of GDP. However, that is an abnormally high figure – even for trend growth of 10% – and so much excess capacity has been built up over the past few years that the government is unlikely to overcome the cuts in capital spending due to market forces. No country has ever sustained investment at 40% of GDP, and Chinese investment should fall to a more normal 30% in spite of government efforts.

Consumption and government constitute only half of China's economy, so would have to grow by 20% to compensate for lost exports and possibly another 10% to compensate for falling investment. The chances of this happening are virtually nil and China's negative demographics will begin to lower its trend growth early in the next decade. Chinese growth is likely to slow far more, and for much longer, than most people now expect. China is quietly joining the trend toward protectionism by imposing non-tariff barriers on foreign products and investment. It is also pushing the creation of new national champions, enterprises that are tied to the government by various ownership structures and enjoy generous financing from the state-owned banks.

Clearly, the world cannot count on Chinese growth to start growth again. India and Russia never were nations that could provide economic leadership, and recent policy errors, such as excessive fiscal and monetary stimulation in India and excessive Russian aggression, ensure they will not be in the foreseeable future. Worse, a populist backlash against globalisation is creating a rising tide of protectionism similar to the one that occurred near the end of the last period of globalisation. The rising emphasis on security will probably accelerate the trend towards protectionism, especially the protection of domestic companies from foreign takeovers.

Constraints on trade will hurt emerging nations that do not succeed in generating enough domestic demand to offset lost exports as much as or more than developed nations. Slowing trade, rising geopolitical tensions and credit difficulties are undoing the benefits globalisation bestowed in the past. The new American government is more protectionist in practice than the previous one, so the current cycle of globalisation has passed its peak and world trade is falling for the first time in a generation. Falling trade will hurt world growth in the future, and unfortunately American and European government panic that the recession and credit problems would cause a replay of the 1930s has initiated moves that will reduce world growth even more.

The Eurasian savings glut was the means by which excess savings in the current account surplus nations, such as the Asian tigers and oil-producing nations, were transferred to current account deficit nations to finance their consumption in excess of production. This vendor financing scheme kept world growth at high levels until consumers in borrow-and-spend nations, mainly Anglo Saxon, ran out of capacity to borrow. Asset prices then fell and household debt delinquency rose, which initiated a credit crunch in the grossly overlevered financial system and a recession. The good news is that current account deficits in borrow-and-spend nations and current account surpluses in save-and-export nations have begun to fall, starting the correction of the saving and investment imbalances caused by the Eurasian savings glut. The bad news is that the correction has a long way to go.

Deleverage has barely begun

There has been considerable hype about deleverage, but it is occurring only in the household sector, and there only because equity in homes is falling fast and accelerating – down 41% from the end of 2005 to the first quarter of 2009. Falling owners' equity in their homes is raising mortgage delinquencies and foreclosures to record high levels month after month. Some 13% of all mortgages were delinquent or in some process of foreclosure at the end of the first quarter of 2009 – far above any previous record.

Losses from loans in foreclosure have risen to an average of 44% and delinquencies in the other forms of consumer credit are setting new records too. Worse credit problems lie ahead because huge numbers of adjustable rate prime and Alt A (those between prime and sub-prime) mortgages come up for renewal in 2010–12. In addition, irresponsible lending also infected commercial real estate, all forms of consumer loans and business loans, especially private equity.

Business defaults had begun to rise by the end of 2008, but they were expected to soar, especially after the recession ended. Business defaults and credit spreads usually peak a year or two after a recession ends, but balance sheets have been so weakened that some credit spreads rose to even wider levels in the recession than had occurred in the Great Depression. The wide spreads probably herald high default rates in business and commercial mortgages too, making significant deleverage in the private non-bank sector inevitable.

The prospect of deleverage conflicts with a consensus, at least in official circles, that borrowing creates wealth. This means the economy cannot delever without causing a depression, so the public sector must offset any tendency for the private sector to delever. If this privatises gains and socialises losses, so be it. That is the price the public must pay to be protected on the downside, so the authorities are doing everything they can to prevent deleverage anywhere in the system.

That consensus is wrong. Chapter 4 showed good credit – that is, transferring saving to borrowers – never creates macro problems, whereas bad credit – that is, borrowing printed money – always leads to credit liquidation. No credit structure can function normally with a big overhang of bad debt, regardless of where it is located. Gearing up created the problem. Gearing down is the solution – and inevitable without government interference. The Fed Senior Loan Officer Survey for the first quarter of 2009 showed the proportion of banks tightening lending standards had abated and the demand for most loans continued to fall. However, the demand for mortgages rose, even though falling house prices and owners' equity in their homes had caused net repayment of mortgage debt in the four quarters prior to the first quarter of 2009.

Total credit continues to grow faster than GDP, as the tiny drop in private non-financial credit growth relative to GDP caused by household debt repayments is being overwhelmed by government borrowing in a desperate attempt to protect overlevered financial institutions. Their excess leverage prohibits them from liquidating assets because the losses on a small amount of their assets would turn their minuscule capital negative and condemn them to winding down. That is the only sensible solution to their problems, but government anxiety over increasing lending has ruled it out.

Financial debt still totals over $17 trillion despite a tiny drop in the first quarter of 2009. The hype said it would create safety by repackaging and redistributing risk according the desire and ability to absorb specific risks. In reality, it only compounded risk and so was counterproductive. Financial institutions with the biggest portfolios of bad assets lent mostly to fund derivatives and other nonproductive purposes. Financial markets will not function properly until this debt has been largely eliminated.

Conclusion

Extremely loose monetary policies and pandering to special interest groups, such as government-sponsored agencies, Wall Street and the City, resulted in the US and Europe gearing up far too much, and excessive credit inflated consumption for over 25 years. The end of the credit cycle had begun to correct unsustainable global imbalances and excess leverage as painlessly as possible. However, exaggerated public perceptions of economic weakness panicked governments in 2007.

The Fed slashed policy rates too soon and far too much, which caused a needless flight from the dollar. The resulting commodities bubble raised inflation rates, which reduced real incomes and spending. The resulting slowdown aggravated household defaults and ended the credit cycle, which, together with the weak growth in

Figure 5.6 **US GDP growth in US$ per additional $ of debt, 1956–2008**

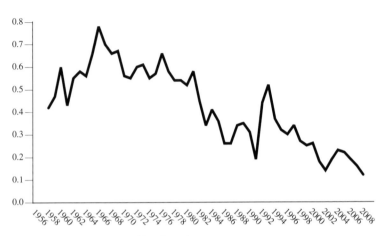

Source: Federal Reserve Board; Lombard Street Research

developed nations, caused a severe global recession. Governments are borrowing to bail out homeowners, financial institutions and non-financial companies. At best, this can only be a short-term fix because the additional growth from a dollar of debt is barely more than enough to pay the interest on the debt.

The amount of GDP produced by an additional dollar of debt falls in recessions and rises in recoveries. Figure 5.6 shows a two-year average which smooths out fluctuations. The downward trend is obvious and the current amount is little above the cost of the added interest, the level where borrowing begins to subtract from GDP rather than add to it. The massive government borrowing will not reinstate prosperity. At best, it will impede investment for the foreseeable future and at worst it will offset the immediate benefits of the fiscal stimulation.

Household and corporate bankruptcies will rise until the private sector has delevered enough to pay its debts on time in the bad times as well as the good – and its creditworthiness will often be tested. The increasingly negative demographics, rising relative costs of food and energy, reversal of globalisation, protectionism, ill-advised environmental policies, current overcapacity and saturated markets mean that average growth in developed nations will rarely be as high as 2% over the next decade or so. Low growth and policy mistakes mean the sovereign creditworthiness of most developed nations will fall for the foreseeable future. Supranational agencies can keep smaller countries viable, but what will happen when a major nation threatens to default is debatable.

Most developed nations face a long battle with the investment decelerator. Japan and, more recently, Germany have staved off the investment decelerator with increasing exports, but now both appear to have lost the battle. Most developed nations will soon find themselves in the same position and the competition to grow by exporting will become ever more severe. Global growth rates will be far lower than in recent years – unless emerging nations replace lost exports to developed nations with domestic demand.

This transition will not be easy as replacing exports with domestic demand does not need the high levels of investment that were required to generate the past high growth in exports. The fall in the rate of growth of investment will combine with negative demographics to lower trend growth in many emerging nations. Their growth will not be enough to enable developing nations to export their way to better growth, so world recessions will become more common.

Even so, the sharpest inventory correction in post-war history combined with the deflation of the food and energy bubble should ignite a recovery. However, Japan's experience shows that policy mistakes after a credit bubble bursts nip recoveries in the bud, even in benign economic environments. Thus the big tax increases already in the pipeline will end the coming recovery before it can become the passport to renewed prosperity. Big losses and economic uncertainties have created great fear in financial markets.

6

Credit and financial markets

The rising demand for credit that began in 2001 was mainly to buy houses and equity. It ended with a final surge in the third quarter of 2007 from private equity and corporate debt for equity swaps (see Figure 6.1). Irresponsible lending and borrowing (not fundamental factors such as inflation and growth) had caused the rise in house and equity prices, and they fell sharply when even totally irresponsible lending and borrowing could not increase credit enough to support the bubbles. Falling house and equity prices together decimated private demand for credit, but tax rebates, government guarantees of bank borrowing and bailouts caused a surge in government borrowing. The statistics show a net repayment in the first quarter of 2009, but that includes double counting in the financial sector as the reduction in financial sector debt outstanding was far less than indicated by the negative borrowing figure.

Tightening lending standards, trashed balance sheets and low growth mean that private non-financial borrowing, the main factor in creating money growth, will remain low to negative for a long time. Lack of demand for credit from creditworthy private borrowers is the main factor negating government efforts to force banks to lend more money. Low private borrowing in the early 1990s (businesses actually repaid loans in 1990 and 1991) caused a sharp drop in money growth (see Figure 6.2). This time the drop in money growth has been taking place in the shadow banks, so official broad

Figure 6.1 **Quarterly US borrowing annualised, 2000–09**

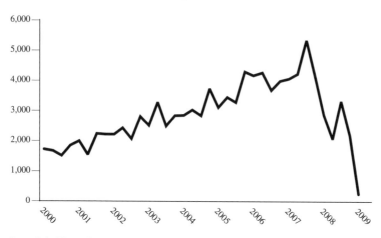

Source: Federal Reserve Board

Figure 6.2 **Year-on-year US M2 growth, 1980–2009**

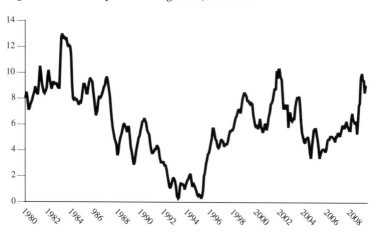

Source: Federal Reserve Board

money growth has not been falling as it has in preceding slowdowns. However, it is important to note that public desire to hold liquidity is limiting the effects of broad money growth.

Confidence and interest rates are the main factors that determine the desire to hold money available on demand (liquidity). Figure 3.8 on page 92 shows the public desire to hold liquidity is on a long-term uptrend and has risen to a record high proportion of GDP – at least since the current money series started in 1959. Holdings of liquidity are high because comparisons with the 1930s shattered confidence and risk-free interest rates fell to record lows. Rising demand for liquidity not only raised risk premiums to levels seen only in the Great Depression, but also prevented lower interest rates from unclogging moribund credit markets. Central banks became lenders of last resort to almost everyone in a continuing effort to free credit markets. They took vast quantities of unmarketable debt onto their books and the extremely wide credit spreads narrowed.

This was heralded as a great achievement but, at best, it is only a stopgap measure. The private non-bank sector must delever before credit markets can function normally. Slashing interest rates not only did not sort out solvency problems, but also caused the commodity inflation that initiated the current recession. It also penalised savers in low saving nations, which must save more to repair their balance sheets and end their solvency problems. Slashing interest rates put monetary authorities in liquidity traps, which occur when policy interest rates close or equal to zero do not stimulate the economy.

Liquidity traps occur because investors fear capital losses on non-money assets and keep their assets in highly liquid, risk-free investments. Fear of default on loans probably causes the most damage because lack of lending to creditworthy borrowers aggravates slowdowns and can initiate deflation. However, extremely low interest rates have no place to go but up, so bond and stock prices are likely to fall and cause capital losses. Japan suffered from a liquidity trap in the 1990s and began a major quantitative easing programme to encourage bank lending to the private sector and so create inflation.

Japanese quantitative easing stimulated private borrowing in several countries, but Japan was not one of them because it lacked willing and creditworthy borrowers. Many nations are now in liquidity traps and are trying to force their banks to lend more. Their efforts will fail too because irresponsible lending and borrowing created a lack of creditworthy borrowers. All forced additional lending can do is add to the problems by funding more irresponsible lending and borrowing.

The diametrically opposed directions of growth in the monetary base and growth in money supply in the three biggest currencies (see Figure 3.1, page 65) show the essence of a liquidity trap is banks hoarding reserves and thereby rendering monetary policy useless. The Fed's chairman, Ben Bernanke, said that if monetary policy failed to stimulate the economy he would drop money from helicopters, hence the nickname Helicopter Ben. Fiscal stimulation is the practical way of fulfilling the helicopter imagery but, as we will see in the next chapter, fiscal stimulation is, at best, a short-term palliative. Fiscal deficits were ineffective in every banking crisis the World Bank studied and they will be ineffective in this crisis too.

Financial markets are reactive

The current, prevalent notion that credit determines spending is false and dangerous. It is false because confidence (supported by the requisite amount of liquidity) and opportunity cost determine spending. It is dangerous because the focus on credit makes it grow faster than GDP, which reduces the quality of the credit and lowers the probability lenders will get their money back. Chapter 3 showed excess liquidity raised asset prices and reduced the quality of credit until the very notion of creditworthiness depended on asset prices rising rather than the ability to pay interest and principal.

The excess liquidity lowered trend growth rates by reallocating resources from investment in plant and equipment to speculation in assets. The credit bubble grossly overpriced assets and then burst when the supply of borrowers, even those who had no hope of meeting their obligations, dried up. The only private-sector borrowers remaining creditworthy had abstained from the speculation and their confidence had vanished before the bubble burst. Their demands on the credit structure are small and will remain so until recovery is firmly established. Left alone, banks in trouble could have run down their balance sheets until they regained control, were merged with stronger banks or were liquidated.

Unfortunately, demands for a pain-free solution to the problems the credit bubble had created panicked the authorities into desperately trying to extend the biggest credit bubble in history. Slashing interest rates and printing money to encourage borrowing are compounding the prior error of keeping interest rates far too low for far too long in the 2002–07 recovery. In effect, central banks are conducting a war against saving – the wrong thing to do in a solvency crisis. Not only are savings double taxed (the income that provided the saving in the first place was taxed), but also the lower interest rates are intended to reduce saving. This is counterproductive in borrow-and-spend nations because now saving is needed both to pay down excess debt and to provide investment.

Worse, markets recognised the official panic and reacted to it. Contrary to popular opinion, financial markets do not forecast. They evaluate the existing psychology and react to it. This evaluation occurs in real time. For example, 90-day Treasury bills traded at 0.01% when commercial banks were paying up to 3% on 90-day term deposits. The US Treasury backs both yields (up to $250,000 for deposits), so the risk of loss is equally non-existent.

The different yields did not forecast different futures for risk-free rates; they measured the hopes and fears of different sets of lenders and borrowers. Treasury bill yields are driven by one set; bank deposit interest is driven by another set. Similarly, 30-year Treasuries yielded less than 3% taxable while some 30-year AAA state and local credits yielded 6% and more tax-free. These markets did not forecast interest rates for 30 years or the default rate of AAA state and local credits. They evaluated the differing group psychology of high-income individuals compared with institutional investors at that time.

The Lehman Brothers collapse in September 2008 turned investor fears into panic and financial markets became extremely volatile. Panic selling lowered prices and then margin calls took over. Forced selling from overlevered long positions unable to post the margins needed to cover the original fall in prices drove them even lower. This triggered more forced selling in a vicious circle that drove valuations to depression levels. For example, US Treasury bills traded at a premium and Treasury bonds traded at considerably lower yields than in the 1930s. Investment grade corporate bond yield spreads from Treasuries exceeded six percentage points, a level previously seen only in the depths of that depression, and junk bonds traded at even higher yields than in the 1930s.

Depression valuations were not rational as the world economy was far from depression. Rising hopes (or greed) had created a quarter of a century of rising risk seeking after the credit crunch ended in 1982. The real estate risk bubble satiated those hopes and they began to reverse into fears in 2006–07. Investor psychology reversing from risk seeking to risk aversion caused the panic flight from risk assets in late 2008. Risk aversion, which increases as overall uncertainty increases, has characterised financial markets for more of history than risk seeking. Slowing global growth should keep uncertainty and risk aversion high.

Risk aversion will rise

The underlying factors are negative for economic growth. Demographic profiles indicate lower potential growth rates everywhere, overcapacity exists in nearly every industry, and consumers in major consuming nations have run out of the capacity to borrow and are now gearing down. Emerging nations can grow relatively quickly through rising domestic demand, but earnings from exporting to developed nations create a significant part of their domestic demand. Lower propensities to import in developed nations are hindering the growth of domestic demand in emerging nations.

Risk aversion should pervade financial markets for much of the next quarter of a century or so. Risk-averse investors worry more about maintaining stable incomes than capital gains, so credit-induced asset booms like those of the past 25 years are unlikely in the next 25. Even so, the panic in financial markets in late 2008 and early 2009 was excessive, and risk markets became grossly oversold and sovereign markets grossly overbought. The collapse of the commodity boom quickly quelled headline inflation, which significantly increased real incomes and savings rates in spite of big rises in unemployment.

The sharp global inventory liquidation in late 2008 and early 2009 will reverse quickly and the fiscal stimulation packages will augment the rising real incomes, so economic figures should surprise on the upside in the second half of 2009 and 2010. Major risk market rises from the late 2008 and early 2009 levels are likely. The undue pessimism will probably reverse into optimism that all the credit problems have been solved and prosperity has returned, but that optimism will be misplaced. We are much less than halfway through the credit difficulties. Tax increases and defaults will abbreviate recoveries and lengthen recessions for the next decade or more, so investment risk will rise.

Many commodity prices fell below the marginal cost of production and had to rise to induce the growing production needed to maintain recovery. Rising commodity prices during the recovery should end the fall in price indexes and the vast amounts of money central banks have printed could fund an explosion in inflation rates. Central banks can cap rising inflation, but they have not done so in the past. A perception that central banks are not doing enough to contain price rises would result in an inflation scare and rising interest rates, even if the perception were in error.

We saw above that little has been done to alleviate the solvency problems, so a relatively small rise in interest rates would cap the recovery – as would inadequate income growth or greater than expected default rates. As a result, the recovery will probably be short-lived and falling prices in the ensuing downturn should initiate significant private non-bank credit liquidation and chronic deflation. However, debt liquidation and deflation should hurt economies far less than feared as their function is to realign asset prices with incomes and output prices, which occurred in the US in 1920–21. Unfortunately, government interference increases the pain and lengthens the period of adjustment, as occurred in America in the 1930s.

The credit boom raised asset prices far more than output growth and the collapse of the shadow banking system has lowered asset prices far more than growth. Some asset prices may be near structural lows but others have further to fall. More importantly, the absence of credit-fuelled booms will shorten recoveries, so expectations of future growth and inflation will change more often, making financial markets more volatile. The feel-bad factor from falling house prices and volatile financial markets will keep risk aversion on an upward trend for a long time.

Investing in fixed income securities

Risk-averse investors favour prime quality securities that produce reliable income flows. The real values of fixed income securities (excluding those indexed to inflation) rise in deflations. The purchasing power of both interest payments and repayment of principal rises as prices fall, making high-quality conventional bonds the optimum risk-averse investment. Fair value for the real yields on longer-term sovereign bonds of major nations has ranged between 2% and 4%, depending on sovereign creditworthiness, monetary policy and national saving relative to investment.

Headline price indexes began to fall in August 2008 and the inflation premium in conventional sovereign bond yields vanished. Safe-haven buying, as investors panicked over deflation and depression, sent the nominal yields on Treasuries and some other sovereign bonds down to their fair value real yields (about equal to their nominal yields because the headline inflation rate was then about zero) in December 2008. The rush into sovereign bonds constituted the last asset bubble in the current series. Thereafter, safe-haven buying lessened and expectations of recovery, inflation and tighter monetary policy kept upward pressure on longer-term sovereign yields up to the time of writing this book.

The cost of voluntary fiscal stimulation, bank guarantees and bailouts is raising both the risk inherent in sovereign bonds and real interest rates, so real yields should rise. Inflation expectations have exceeded actual inflation, so investors have been overpricing inflation protection. Safe-haven buying in the 2007–08 inflation scare sent the yields of inflation-protected bonds (IPB) far below fair value in most jurisdictions. However, Treasury Inflation Protected Securities (TIPS) yields and other sovereign IPB yields rose sharply in the deflation scare that followed the inflation scare.

Buyers of outstanding IPB pay sellers the accumulated inflation protection from the issue date to the settlement date, so are at risk from deflation after the purchase. This means the total return on IPB may be less than the purchase yield to maturity. However, the total return will have maintained constant purchasing power – the intended purpose of the bond.

Figure 6.3 **Yields of 30-year TIPS versus real 30-year Treasury, 1998–2009**

Source: Federal Reserve Board

TIPS indicate real interest rates better than conventional Treasuries because the yields on the latter embody expectations of the future inflation rate, which vary far more than expectations for real yields. Sharply falling inflation expectations pushed the real yields of conventional Treasuries below the real yields of TIPS in 2000, 2005 and 2008 (see Figure 6.3). Then the actuality of sharply falling inflation rates sent the real yields on conventional bonds above TIPS yields. The important point is that financial engineering increased the desire to lend relative to the desire to borrow from the turn of the century to 2005, enabling the Eurasian savings glut to push down real interest rates rather than incomes. Financial engineering reached its zenith in 2005 and real interest rates trended upwards thereafter.

The lower ability of the US and European non-bank private sector to borrow is reducing trade deficits and imported saving (see Figure 2.4 on page 46), and central banks are inhibiting domestic saving with record low interest rates. By contrast, soaring fiscal deficits are creating much bigger demands on saving. Quantitative easing may fill the gap while the economy is weak, but will only compound funding problems if the economy recovers. Government borrowing is not sensitive to interest rates, but private borrowing is, so real interest rates will rise in the coming recovery and crowd out enough private-sector borrowing to fund the deficits. Output growth will be minimal as a result.

Few appreciate how deep a hole some governments have dug for themselves. For example, President Obama's budget plan triples the US debt held by the public and this is before addressing the explosion in social security and Medicare and Medicaid costs. Peter Orszag, director of the White House Office of Management and Budget, estimates that the costs of Medicare and Medicaid will rise from 5% of GDP to 20% in 2050 if the costs per enrollee do not change. Medical leaders met the President and pledged to cut the projected growth in national health-care spending by 1½ percentage points. That would reduce Medicare and Medicaid costs to 10% of GDP in 2050, but few pledges to cut government costs have produced any saving.

Income taxes will have to rise 13% to pay social security costs in perpetuity. Add in Medicare, and the required rise in income taxes soars to 81%. These unfunded liabilities total $106 trillion, more than double total US private net worth.[30] Halving Medicare costs would drop the required rise in income taxes to 47%, still an extremely worrisome figure.

America is not alone. The UK budget deficit for 2009/10 is 12.4% of GDP, only slightly less than the American deficit, and unlike the US, the drop for the following year is a minuscule 0.5% of GDP. As in the US, taxes are budgeted to rise significantly, by 2.8% of national income in fiscal 2013/14. The Office of National Statistics estimates government injections into Lloyds TSB and RBS could raise public-sector debt to as much as 100% of GDP, and the Institute for Fiscal Studies estimates Britain's debt will not fall back to sustainable levels for 23 years. Fiscal deficits in Russia, Japan,

Spain and Ireland also exceed 10% of GDP, and debt to GDP ratios threaten to spiral out of control in many developed nations.

Japan's experience shows that burgeoning debt will weigh down ageing populations far more than debt ever did in the past. Credit markets have been ambivalent about deteriorating sovereign credit so far. Even though we do not know when they will react to deteriorating credit, we can be reasonably sure sovereign yields will not fall much below the 2008 lows in borrow-and-spend nations. More importantly, spreads from sovereign bonds to high-quality corporate bonds should continue to narrow and ultimately reverse in at least some nations.

Companies with strong balance sheets and good cash flows will thrive in the low inflation to deflationary environment in prospect for many years. Record issuance of investment grade corporate paper has kept spreads from sovereign bonds near Depression levels, but debt markets have been closed to less than investment grade companies.

Yields on junk bonds soared to 25% in late 2008, which, apart from liquidity considerations, implied a 21% default rate. That was an overreaction to officials comparing the present situation to the 1930s, and yields have since halved. They are now far too narrow to compensate for the coming high default rates, the low recovery rates, the illiquidity and the high rate of refinancing in the next few years. Investors lacking distressed bond expertise venture into this market at their peril. Rising risk aversion will greatly reduce the number of junk bonds outstanding in a few years.

Markets for syndicated loans have also been moribund as the S&P/LSTA (Loan Syndication and Trading Association) index of loans traded below 60% of face value before recovering to the high 70s. Loans rank ahead of bonds in a bankruptcy, so even the high 70s seems like a low price, but the LSTA contains levered loans. Recent defaults in levered loans indicate a 25% recovery rate and, as we have seen, credit problems will persist for a long time, default rates will be high and a resumption of former trend growth is unlikely to bail out troubled debtors. Bargains undoubtedly exist in syndicated loans, but distressed finance is a minefield for the unwary.

Structured finance and derivatives have created major problems

As we saw in Chapter 3, most of the loans and credit card debt available in financial markets are in the form of securitised debt. Most securitised debt trust deeds prohibit changing the terms of the constituent loans. This is frustrating attempts to work out suitable terms for householders in difficulty. In addition, many of the securitisations were highly levered, complex and opaque CDO. The CDO business model failed in the 1990s and again in 2007 because the investment banks that priced the debt and the agencies that rated it used badly flawed models. First, the data fed into the models covered only a short time span in which asset prices soared. Rising asset prices were built into the models, so falling asset prices invalidated them. Second, the models can assess only exogenous risk even though endogenous risk can be far greater.

Endogenous risk consists of liquidity risk and counterparty risk. Liquidity risk is the risk of being unable to execute transactions at prices acceptable to both sides. Counterparty risk is the risk that one party to the transaction will fail to meet its commitment. Shocks bombard financial markets continuously. Markets adjust to these shocks without much dislocation when leverage is low because the volume of trading needed to make the adjustments remains within normal ranges and endogenous risk is low.

Higher leverage requires a bigger volume of trade to make the needed adjustments and higher levered counterparties are more likely to fail to meet their commitments. Rising leverage multiplies endogenous risk. Woody Brock has calculated that 30 times leverage is 25 times as risky as 10 times leverage. Global leverage was so high in 2007–08 that endogenous risk accounted for three-quarters of the total risk in financial markets – and the model builders had ignored it. The highly vaunted value-at-risk models used to assess and manage risk ignored up to three-quarters of the risk and their limited databases condemned the models to doing a poor job of assessing the balance.

Excessive leverage intensifies virtually all credit problems, so regulating leverage is by far the most important part of regulating financial institutions and markets. Proper regulation of leverage would keep credit cycles under control and so would have avoided the global current credit problems. For example, Canadian bank regulations limit leverage to 20 times net tangible equity, and as a result Canadian banks are now the strongest in the world. However, limiting leverage encourages banks to make riskier loans, so credit quality must be regulated too.

Excess leverage, much higher than expected default rates and the general use of floating rate coupons on CDO debt in an era of falling short-term rates drastically reduced the prices of CDO. Synthetic CDO fell more than cash CDO as the underlying CDS premiums were woefully underpriced. Not only has the total amount of CDO and synthetic CDO issued fallen by over 95%, but also central banks hold all the CDO issued in 2008 under various bailout schemes.

Issuance of other 'alphabet soup' structured finance products, such as special investment vehicles and constant proportion debt obligations, has virtually ceased. Irresponsible lending, complex and opaque securities, unwarranted high ratings and excess leverage were basic factors in the credit bubble and its subsequent collapse. Structured finance not only embodies all four, but also has been a big obstacle to deleverage progressing smoothly.

Covered bonds avoid the problems inherent in structured finance. Their structures are simple and transparent. The credit risk remains with the originating lender, who is also responsible for resolving problem loans, thus avoiding both irresponsible lending and obstacles to deleverage. Unfortunately, sovereign guarantees of bank bonds eliminated covered bond issuance in many nations because they do not qualify for the guarantees. Banks are starting to issue bonds without guarantees again and, in the absence of another credit crisis, the issuing of covered bonds should soon follow and ultimately minimise the issuance of structured finance vehicles.

Derivatives have been tarred with the same brush as structured finance because some embody great leverage. The total amount of derivatives outstanding rose by 24% a year for the ten years up to June 2008, but the size of and risks in derivative markets have been greatly overstated. The notional amount outstanding counts each side of a trade separately and the only way to change a derivative position is to enter into a new contract that will also be double counted.

The extensive double counting makes the net exposure a small fraction of the total amount outstanding. Also, 64% of the derivatives outstanding are interest rate swaps or options. Swaps exchange, for a defined period of time, a fixed rate of interest for a rate that floats with the changes of a specified short-term interest rate, so they embody little risk of big losses of capital. The purchase price is the total risk in an option, so the capital risk in them is small too.

Even so, some derivatives embody high leverage and high risk, such as CDS, which created lender pay credit insurance. Borrower pay credit insurance had been available since 1971. Lender pay insurance became so popular that CDS were the fastest growing derivatives up to the end of 2007, at which time they constituted 8.6% of all derivatives. However, the CDS business model was flawed because desperation for income streams motivated sellers of credit insurance far more than desire for insurance-motivated buyers. Thus only grossly underpriced premiums could create the volume the sellers wanted. This proved to be costly when the credit crunch exposed the underpricing, and the amounts outstanding began to fall in 2008.

The Depository Trust and Clearing Corporation (DTCC) listed nearly all CDS on its books. The outstanding amount fell by almost

60% from the Bank of International Settlements (BIS) figure at end of 2007 to the DTCC figure of $25 trillion on 13 March 2009. CDS remain the most feared derivatives, even though the amounts outstanding were more than halved with far less trouble than expected. The DTCC is settling CDS claims in credit events by a sophisticated matching of offsetting positions. Estimated CDS losses on the Lehman Brothers default ranged up to $270 billion, but the net payments from credit insurance sellers to buyers were only $5.2 billion, and the net payments on the takeover of Washington Mutual (the biggest credit event in the savings and loan industry) were only $1.3 billion.

Private negotiations have also wound up CDS. Ambac and Citigroup reached an agreement whereby Ambac paid Citigroup $850 million to terminate about $1.4 billion of a CDS referencing a CDO² transaction. Other agreements to terminate CDS have been reported with payouts as low as 13 cents on the dollar. These transactions can be major positives for insurers. Ambac had written the Citigroup position down by $1 billion, so the company not only books a $150 million gain, but also shows it is valuing its liabilities conservatively and should not suffer big mark-to-market losses in the future.

CDS have not caused the Armageddon feared, but they have disrupted financial markets. The total amount of CDS outstanding has been a big multiple of the total amount of the reference debt outstanding. The huge size of the CDS market relative to the bond and loan markets has multiplied volatility in the latter. Arbitraging the grossly underpriced CDS premiums drove credit spreads in cash markets to absurdly low levels until the credit bubble collapsed. Then insurance premiums soared and the resulting undoing and reversing of those arbitrages drove credit spreads to absurdly high levels. Volatility will remain far too high until the amount of CDS outstanding is limited to the amount of reference debt outstanding.

Furthermore, premiums have not covered the losses from credit events, so portfolio sales to cover the losses disrupted fragile financial markets. Lender pay credit insurance can be a valuable financial hedge, but the current CDS business model needs changing. There is no economic reason to insure debts not owing to the insured, so CDS outstanding should not exceed the reference debt outstanding. This flaw can be fixed easily by requiring delivery of the reference debt to collect an insurance claim. CDS will continue to disrupt financial markets until regulators make this rule change and also involve borrowers in the insurance process to ensure conformity to the new rule. CDS are not the only derivatives that distorted financial markets.

The disruptive effects of commodity futures must be stopped

The rise and fall in many commodity prices in the past couple of years has been both unprecedented and co-ordinated, even though the prices of some of the commodities normally fluctuate with growth and/or inflation and others do not.

The only rational explanation for these anomalies is that the highly levered derivatives have overwhelmed cash commodity markets in the same way that CDS disrupted bond and loan markets. Over-the-counter commodity futures outstanding (excluding gold) soared at a 156% annual rate in the first half of 2008. In addition, regulators have multiplied the big leverage already embodied in commodity futures by giving some speculators the right to use margins intended only for hedging the receipt or delivery of the physical product.

The result of this largesse was investment demand causing a commodity boom that raised inflation enough to create the 2007–09 recession. Commodity futures are important for hedging risk, but using futures to speculate on commodity prices with hedging margins has created totally unacceptable volatility in cash commodity prices. Just reversing the rule change that let speculators use margins meant for hedging may be enough to restore the proper functioning of commodity futures markets. If not, regulators will have to raise speculative margins until investment demand can no longer dictate cash price levels.

Precious metals are basically commodities and suffer from the same derivative tail wagging the cash dog as other commodities. Unlike other commodities, however, existing supplies vastly exceed annual demand and this overhead supply moderates price fluctuations. The relative prices of precious metals rise and fall with investor confidence. Confidence was extremely low as the credit crunch began in 1980 and the price of an ounce of gold equalled the Dow Jones Industrial Average (DJIA). Confidence rocketed when the credit crunch was over. Gold prices plummeted and equity prices soared and it took 42 ounces of gold to equal the DJIA in 2000.

Losses from defaults broke through the 1990s highs in 1999, indicating the spike in defaults in the early 1990s was not a one-off. Geopolitical tensions, competition from emerging nations and deflation also threaten the physical, economic and financial security of industrial nations and confidence has plummeted. Gold has risen and the DJIA has fallen since 2000; 8 ounces of gold equalled the DJIA in March 2009.

Recovery may raise the number of ounces of gold needed to equal the DJIA, but the longer-term trend remains downward, even though derivatives threaten the traditional safe-haven role of precious metals. Precious metals became a speculative favourite in the 2002–07 bull market, and low margin derivatives multiplied the demand. The prices of precious metals held up far better than many other investments in 2008, but opportunistic selling to fund margin calls on worse performing assets pushed the prices of precious metals down. This fall in prices meant precious metals only partially fulfilled their role as a safe haven.

Low annual additions to stocks give precious metals a quasi-monetary quality. Their real prices are relatively stable over long periods, so they provide protection from both inflation and deflation.

However, they do not provide incomes, so rising real incomes from the coupons of high-quality, long-term non-callable bonds will make them better investments than precious metals for long-term investors in the coming deflation. Now it is time to turn to higher risk investing. We will look at higher risk investment management before going on to the investments themselves.

Hedge funds and private equity: back to the niche

The diversity of hedge funds is too great to give a meaningful general description of them. Besides, their effect on financial markets is far more important than their design. The two main results of their rapid growth were higher fees and higher leverage. They grew rapidly because investors became ever more willing to pay higher fees in an effort to maintain double-digit returns on their portfolios as income from mainstream investments fell far below expectations and budgets. High gearing on low yields could produce the needed double-digit returns while asset prices were rising and credit was both unduly cheap and easily available. However, leverage works both ways.

The rapid growth of hedge funds eroded both their higher returns and their claims to less correlation with other investments. Then asset prices fell, the credit bubble burst and credit became neither unduly cheap nor easily available. Hedge funds had to post more margin or be sold out. Overextended funds could not meet margin calls and so had to liquidate assets. The forced selling pushed asset prices lower, triggering another round of margin calls and still lower prices in a vicious downward spiral. Not all hedge funds were highly levered, but many were. An estimated 108 imploded in 2007–08 and others had to delay or stop redemptions.

Few managers can consistently produce market-beating results, so the hedge fund business model is, by definition, a niche product.

Figure 6.4 **S&P 500 reported earnings yields less BBB corporate yields, 1988–2009**

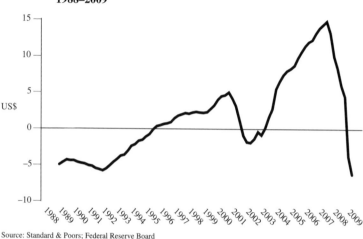

Source: Standard & Poors; Federal Reserve Board

Lending standards are tightening and credit is unlikely to become either cheap or easily available for a long time. The lower returns and leverage that will characterise financial markets in the future will allow mainstream funds with their far lower fees to give better returns than most hedge funds. Hedge funds will keep closing until they become a niche product once again.

The outlook for private equity is similar. Figure 6.4 shows that rates of return on equity ranged up to 15 percentage points above Moody's BBB corporate bond average during the private equity boom. Huge gaps between reported earnings yields and interest rates, as well as the benign forecasts for the future, encouraged managements to borrow funds to buy back their own stock – over $600 billion of it in both 2006 and 2007. Other companies paid big dividends, engaged in mergers and acquisitions, even split up, to raise their debt/equity ratios.

Private equity companies gained enormous profits from buying and levering up companies that did not use any of these techniques to gear up their balance sheets. The private equity business model is to buy companies with relatively stable cash flows and low debt ratios, gear them up and sell them. Much of the added debt merely pays the private equity company big dividends, so the target company's credit rating often sinks several notches. This is basically legal theft from careless bond buyers. It downgrades existing bonds without clauses in their trust deeds protecting holders from losses resulting from premature repayment, ownership changes or material changes in the business. It also greatly raises the odds of default, especially where mergers and acquisitions had created a lot of worthless good will.

Private equity profits depended on cheap and easily available credit, careless bond buyers and the buyers of the resold companies not demanding lower price/earnings ratios to compensate for the greater risk inherent in the higher gearing. However, the end of the credit cycle negated all the conditions that favoured private equity. Equity returns have plummeted far below the cost of borrowing; lending standards have tightened dramatically; bond buyers are now insisting on indentures forcing new majority owners of the company to compensate them for any losses resulting from their actions; and equity buyers are becoming more wary of investing in overlevered companies. Conditions will never again be as favourable to private equity as they were from 2004 to 2007.

Furthermore, many private equity companies face funding gaps because they committed to buy companies based on the expected receipts from the sales of companies they owned. However, sales fell through when credit conditions tightened and equity prices fell, so some private equity companies could not fulfil their commitments. Funding gaps will keep plaguing private equity companies until lending standards loosen or equity markets rise significantly. Even then, the enormous returns on equity relative to the cost of debt in the credit bubble are unlikely to return. Private equity will always be able to replace dozy management but, lacking the returns available in the credit bubble, private equity will return to being a niche player in financial markets.

Higher risk investments

The serial asset booms drove the prices of risk assets (including housing, which acts like a risk asset because of the high ratio of debt usually used to fund the purchase price) far too high relative to incomes and the prices of goods and services. The end of the credit cycle began adjusting this imbalance by hurting financial markets far more than the economy. A recovery will probably interrupt this necessary adjustment, but the adjustment will continue in the next slowdown.

The huge drop in net worth (see Chapter 3) caused by the end of the credit cycle has initiated a steep rise in bankruptcies. In addition, recovery rates are low and likely to go lower as default rates rise. The part of defaulted debt lenders cannot recover in bankruptcy proceedings impairs their equity capital, so the equity of many financial institutions has become badly impaired. Lending standards have tightened greatly as a result. Falling asset prices, tightening lending standards and rising defaults have turned the greed that fuelled the credit bubble into fear.

Chapter 4 showed that emotions drive financial markets. Stock markets are the best barometer of investor emotions because they give continuous readings in real time. The value of a common stock is the present value of its future earnings. Hopes create bull markets by exaggerating the prospects for future earnings and minimising potential risks. Stock prices then incorporate this optimistic picture by raising the multiples of visible earnings. Fears create bear markets by minimising the prospects for future earnings and exaggerating potential risks. Stock prices then incorporate this dismal picture into lower multiples of visible earnings.

Interest rates can affect the course of bull and bear markets. Rising interest rates raise the rate at which future earnings are discounted and so lower stock prices. Similarly, falling interest rates raise stock prices. The average rise in the DJIA was 1% a year during the long-lasting rise in interest rates from 1960 to 1982, compared with 11% a year during the long-lasting fall from 1982 to 2007. Even though central banks manipulate interest rates to control money growth, money growth affected the DJIA differently in the two time frames. The coefficient of correlation between growth in the money supply and equity price changes was 0.37 from 1960 to 1982 and minus 0.23 from 1982 to 2007. Money growth influenced the variation in stock prices according to theory in the first period, but not in the second.

Even though rationalisations abound for every random movement in stock prices, no exogenous factor shows a consistent correlation with stock prices over time. For example, US corporate profits rose over 7% a year from the fourth quarter of 1961 to the second quarter of 1982 and again from the second quarter of 1982 to the first quarter of 2000. However, the DJIA rose only 0.5% a year in the first time period and a massive 15% a year in the second, torpedoing the theory that profits determine the course of stock markets in any time frame meaningful to investors.

Endogenous factors (for which read group psychology) are the root cause of all the changes in financial markets. For example, US inflation rates rose sharply immediately after the Second World War, yet US interest rates fell to all-time lows because group psychology was extremely bearish. Most people were expecting a post-war depression. By contrast, interest rates rose with the rising inflation from 1960 to 1982 because most people feared inflation and interest rates would keep rising indefinitely. Group psychology, not rising inflation, caused the rise in interest rates. Fear that rising interest rates would erode stock prices limited their average annual rise to one-fifteenth of the annual rise in profits. The trend in personal savings rates supports this analysis.

Figure 6.5 **Real DJIA versus personal savings rate inverted, 1959–2009**

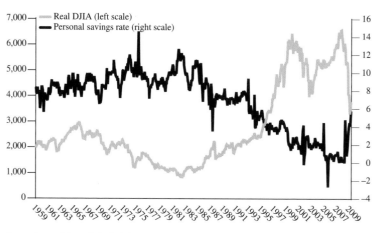

Source: Bureau of Economic Analysis; Lombard Street Research

Rising levels of fear caused rising personal savings rates and the fall in real equity prices up to 1982 (see Figure 6.5 and note the reversed scale for the savings rate). Rising levels of hope that ultimately turned into greed caused falling personal savings rates and the rise in real equity prices from 1982 to 2000. Investors saved Microsoft's outsized dividend in 2004 and the lack of a repeat one year later caused an equal and opposite statistical aberration. Apart from that, the fear that initiated the stock market fall in late 2007 also started a rise in the savings rate from its lowest levels a few months later. The real prices of US equities fell to 1996 levels, even though real GDP has risen by one-third.

Rising hopes in the boom gave rise to unrealistic expectations, such as that of creating value with mergers and acquisitions (M&A). Various studies have shown that more than 50% of mergers fail to create value. One study found 83% of mergers failed to create value and half actually destroyed value. Surprisingly, polling the boards of the companies involved in those mergers showed over 80% of the board members thought (or wished) their acquisitions had created value.[31]

The need to write off vast amounts of worthless goodwill since M&A became popular shows it often destroys rather than creates value – and the studies considered value for shareholders only. Nearly all M&A reduces bondholders' equity through lower credit ratings, making them economic negatives. M&A and private equity not only misallocated resources but also forced other companies to gear up too much to fend off the predators. That gearing up is the main reason defaults will soar in the next few years.

The shrinkage of M&A, hedge funds and private equity will greatly reduce the demand for equities for many years. Also, M&A has produced a plethora of companies, especially in the financial industry, that are considered 'too big to fail' and so must be bailed out. However, the bailouts are consolidating them into even bigger companies, which will create even more systemic risk by becoming 'too big to bail out'. Fear of a catastrophic failure will rise until break-ups, spin-offs and divestitures start to rationalise the size of companies.

M&A, private equity and company stock buy-backs constituted a major equity-for-debt swap, so the amount of equity outstanding plummeted. This raised per-share profits for many years. Now, low growth and deflation caused by the end of the credit cycle are pushing sales and profits below budget and raising the burden of that debt. Many companies that avidly bought equity at the top of the market are now over levered and trying to sell equity at half of or less than the prices at the high. In an editorial in the *Wall Street Journal* in April 2009, Mike Milken wrote that corporate credit problems are largely self-inflicted and many companies now struggling would have had little debt if they had not repurchased equity.

Solvent companies are trying to lower their interest costs by issuing equity. Less solvent companies are asking creditors to take equity in exchange for their loans. Insolvent companies are default-ing – except those that are too big to fail. Governments intend to rescue those at any price, including rewriting contract law. The government-mandated Chrysler bankruptcy settlement gave junior creditors bigger payouts – government 80% and unions 50% – than senior creditors (30%). The extraordinary sale to Fiat on government-dictated terms prevents senior creditors from voting on the settle-ment, which they could have done in a bankruptcy court. Settlement by political favouritism will increase the costs of corporate borrow-ing for a long, long time.

Deflation and the issuance of massive amounts of stock will lower the long-term rate of growth in the return on equity. Real equity prices in the US have risen at a trend rate of about 2½% since 1871, compared with real economic growth of about 3½%, largely because management has owned an ever lower proportion of stock. Divorcing management and ownership has allowed executives to greatly dilute shareholder rights and manage companies as their private fiefdoms rather than for the benefit of shareholders. Increasing shareholder rights is a necessary step in improving the quality of management.

Reinvested dividends raised the real return on equity to about 6.7%, so they have provided over 60% of the return on equity. Tiny dividend yields in recent years and the collapse in stock prices that wiped out $37 trillion of equity from October 2007 to March 2009 pushed the total real return on equity down to over 40% below trend. Only the First World War, the Great Depression, the Second World War, the Korean war and the credit crunch of the 1980s pushed total returns on equity further below trend.

Stocks should be cheap at these low levels, but other measures indicate they will become cheaper. Equity prices range from about eight times normalised earnings at the bottom of bear markets to about 20 times at the top of bull markets. The recent extreme vola-tility in earnings makes it hard to estimate normalised earnings. Applying the average long-term growth rate of 2½% to the ten-year average earnings in March 2009 gives a normalised price/earnings ratio of 15, the long-term average. Stock prices could halve from March 2009 levels, but that is unlikely.

We are probably halfway through the bear market that began in 2000 and halfway through the transition from hope to fear. Huge write-offs probably made average reported earnings in the fourth quarter of 2008 worse than any to come. Operating earnings may also have hit the bottom, but we do not have the pessimism that reigns supreme at the bottom of bear markets. The lowest price/earnings ratios occur after profits have risen significantly, so lower price/ earnings multiples do not guarantee lower prices. The March 2009 lows may prove to be the lowest prices in this cycle, but, sporadic rallies notwithstanding, a new bull market is highly unlikely in the next few years. A range-bound market trading between the 2007 highs and 2009 lows is much more likely.

Rob Arnott's Research Affiliates showed that if sovereign bonds are rolled over every year they can outperform stocks over long periods of time.[32] The total return on bonds equalled or exceeded the total return on stocks for the 68 years 1803–71, the 20 years 1929–49 and the 41 years 1968–2009. Stocks greatly outperformed bonds for significant periods within those time spans, but the important point is that sovereign bond returns can beat equity returns over long periods of time if inflation is near zero, falling or negative. Contrary to current market expectations, high-grade bond returns are likely to match or exceed equity returns over the several years needed to repair private-sector balance sheets.

The rate of return on bonds relative to the rate of return on equities depends on investors' expectations of the volatility of bond prices relative to the volatility of equity prices. The record volatility of equity prices and lower volatility in bond prices in recent years have pushed investors into demanding much higher returns from equities. Figure 6.4 on page 159 shows the S&P 500 equity earnings yield is currently far below the Moody's BBB average bond yield.

This means investment grade company bonds should yield higher returns than their equities over the next five or ten years. Commodities are a poor long-term investment too.

Commodities are not an investment class

The steep rises in commodity prices from 1999 to 2008 persuaded many investors that commodities are an investment class – even though rising productivity has reduced the real prices of commodities throughout history. Declining real prices make commodities poor investments. However, Chapter 1 showed that real energy, water and food prices are likely to rise. The big rise in finding and development costs in recent years should keep the real price of oil on a flat to rising trend. Even so, the uncertainty of its valuation and price volatility make oil a speculation rather than an investment. The Credit Suisse report discussed in Chapter 1 shows that small differences in input assumptions create big variations in the equilibrium price of oil.

Private ownership of water is rare and encumbered with riparian rights, so water is not suitable for direct investment. Agricultural prices are volatile and weather dependent, so agricultural products are also unsuitable as investments. In addition, the big commodity bubble is over and another one is unlikely for three reasons:

- Rising risk aversion is eliminating commodities as an investment class, so investment demand will not be a big factor in the future.
- The high industrial commodity prices reduced demand through a combination of substitution (plastic for copper in plumbing, for instance), economising and lower growth.
- Emerging nations are providing most of, if not all, the added demand for commodities. Their low incomes cannot absorb big price increases as well as high western incomes and some, especially

China, are trying to implement less commodity-intensive growth models.

The real estate correction is far from over

Real estate was the final bubble in the credit cycle. Many nations greatly overbuilt both commercial and residential real estate. Slowing to negative growth in labour forces is curbing the growth in housing and retail demand in most developed nations. More importantly, the unrealistic hopes that rising real estate prices would provide painless saving for retirement have not only evaporated, but are also turning into fears that are reducing investment in real estate. In 2008, US building permits fell to the lowest annual rate since records began in 1960 – and then kept falling.

A combination of federal, state and bank programmes were implemented in 2008 to reduce foreclosures. Some of their provisions even contravened contract law, yet foreclosure filings rose in 2008 to 3.2 million on 2.3 million properties. (Some properties have more than one mortgage and each one requires a separate filing.) This was the highest annual total ever, an 81% increase on 2007 and a 225% increase on 2006. The rise continues as April 2009 showed the highest monthly total of foreclosure activity ever. About 160,000 foreclosure sales usually occur in a year, but now about 80,000 occur each month. Distressed properties accounted for half the sales of existing houses in March 2009 and will continue to do so for a long time, dragging prices lower.

Furthermore, the peak of the adjustable rate mortgage resets does not occur until mid-2011, so we are only about 40% of the way through the mortgage problems. Unemployment is a lagging indicator and will keep rising for another year or so, adding to the losses in consumer debt and mortgages. Even so, investor fears were still in the embryonic stage in late 2008 in the US as 51% of Americans then believed it was a good time to buy a house in spite of an esti-mated 12 million homeowners, a quarter of those with mortgages, having negative equity in their homes.

Slowing demand and rising fears of deflation will greatly lower and probably eliminate the break-even inflation rate embedded in house prices. Renting real estate involves direct costs for manage-ment, repairs and taxes. Indirect costs include vacancies, transaction costs, damage by tenants, opportunity costs because of illiquidity and the risk of loss on resale. These costs should make rental yields a few percentage points higher than mortgage rates, but rental yields generally have been lower than mortgage rates. Capital gains have compensated for the inadequate income from rents.

For example, suppose you use a 7% mortgage to pay $200,000 for a house and rent it for $12,000 a year with total costs of $4,000 a year. The rental yield is 6%, less than the mortgage rate – a typical situation. Net income is only $8,000 compared with the $14,000 you pay on the $200,000 mortgage, so the price of the house must rise for you to break even. An average rise of 4% a year would let you break even in 18 years and give a small profit at the end of a 20-year mortgage. If you want the net earnings to pay the 7% mortgage, you can pay only $114,000 for the house. The assumed break-even infla-tion rate of 4% a year created a 75% inflation premium in the price of the house.

Falling house prices are reducing the inflation premium in house prices, but there is still a long way to go. Real estate prices in many nations doubled in real terms from the mid-1990s to the mid-2000s to around twice 'fair value'. The correction so far has removed about half the overvaluation, but prices usually overcorrect before stabilis-ing near fair value, so the real estate correction has a long way to go. *Caveat emptor*!

Currencies

Lack of banking facilities, trade restrictions, exchange controls and exchange rate manipulation have kept the currencies of mercantilist emerging nations undervalued relative to those of the big developed nations – including the dollar. The US abrogated its responsibilities as host to the world's reserve currency with President Johnson's famous 'guns and butter' programme in the 1960s. This led President Nixon to end the Bretton Woods Agreement by shutting the gold window in 1971. The general perception that the dollar has been in a sustained downtrend ever since is mistaken (see Figure 2.3 on page 44).

Nevertheless, that perception combined with US irresponsibility has led to continuous questioning of the dollar's status as a reserve currency. Many people believed, or at least hoped, the euro could replace the dollar as a reserve currency. Foreign exchange reserves held in euros rose to 25% of the total in 2003, but the innate weaknesses of the euro have limited that rise ever since – in spite of the US problems. Euro-zone nations lack the commonality required for an effective political union, they lack the mobility of labour and capital needed for an effective currency union, and they have far less ability to transfer funds from prosperous to struggling areas than the US.

Euro-zone nations have traded all monetary and significant fiscal sovereignty for currency stability. Chapter 4 showed the attraction of this trade, but the nations that formerly had a weak currency policy to boost exports and limit imports have not adjusted to the euro-zone's strong currency regime. Euro-zone nations that had pursued a strong currency policy to keep inflation down and promote productivity are unlikely to acquiesce to a weak currency policy. Low growth and deflation will inflame desires to secede, but secession is far more complicated – and will achieve far less – than most people think. Current fears of secession are overstated as it would be a long-drawn-out process.

However, recent statements negating the no-bailout clause make it likely that a euro-zone nation in default would remain in the euro. Uncertainty of what this really means is also raising questions about the euro. The chances of the euro replacing the dollar as the reserve currency in the foreseeable future are almost nil. A quarter or more of the world's reserves will remain in euros until either defaults or secession create much greater problems than now exist. However, that does not indicate exchange rate stability. Greater volatility will pervade foreign exchange markets because the lower growth rates will increase both hopes and fears about the viability of many nations and currency markets will reflect all these emotional changes.

The synchronised global slowdown pushed the dollar up, but the stimulus bill, the prospect of large and continuing quantitative easing and the focus on US unfunded liabilities reversed the dollar's rise. This has reignited resistance to US efforts to devalue the dollar – a clear violation of the obligations of a reserve currency. Chapter 2 showed China will keep currency reform on the agenda, but meaningful action is unlikely before conditions deteriorate considerably.

Interest rates affected the prices of floating currencies more and more as credit conditions eased. Tightening credit conditions will make current account balances a bigger factor in currency prices. Currencies of nations with reliable current account surpluses, such as Switzerland, should trend upwards, but a continuing good credit standing will be required to maintain the upward trend. International allocation of reserves to yen, which have been falling because of low interest rates, will rise even though Japanese current account surpluses have become far less reliable than people thought. Allocations to the yuan could become significant, but only if it becomes freely tradable and Chinese current account surpluses persist. The chances of both these events occurring are less than most people think.

Currencies of nations with big current account deficits, such as the US, should trend down – regardless of high credit rating or interest rates. International allocation of reserves to sterling, which have been rising because of its high interest rates, should fall along with the price of sterling. Fiscal stimulation, bailouts, bank guarantees and recapitalisations are devaluing many currencies. This should stop, and ultimately reverse, the liquidation of gold held in foreign exchange reserves.

Conclusion

Franklin Roosevelt said in his inaugural address in 1933: 'We have nothing to fear but fear itself.' Economic conditions today are infinitely better than in 1933, but the fear factor has arguably been as great. The panic displayed by central banks and in financial markets has led to far bigger losses than necessary and these, in turn, have led to needless fears of economic ruin.

Asset prices had risen far too high relative to incomes and output prices. Correction of that imbalance is forcing the entire financial industry to correct. The total income of US financial companies, including real estate, grew by almost 60%, from 13% of the national total to almost 21%. Their shares of industry profits and industry employees grew proportionately. Financial industries in other industrial nations have shown a similar performance. The period of outsized returns is over. Lower returns will cut a lot of fat out of an industry that has added greatly to costs and little to returns. Official panic to stop the correction is greatly extending its duration.

Emerging nations' banking systems are maturing and reducing their need to channel funds through industrial nations' financial systems. Fearful investors trade less than risk-seeking investors and the rising proportion of retirees consume savings rather than add to them, so their needs for financial services will fall too. The big profits from increasing leverage are gone, which will minimise leveraged buy-out and private equity deals that made money from leverage rather than economic contribution. Future profits will have to be earned.

Derivatives played far less of a role in the credit bubble and its collapse than structured finance. Proper regulation should correct the flaws in rogue derivatives, enabling them to play their proper role in distributing and hedging risk. By contrast, structured finance played a big role in the credit bubble and crash by aiding the irresponsible lending and borrowing that trashed household balance sheets – the basic foundation of the credit structure. Structured finance was also a big factor in raising financial leverage far above any previous level, and it created securities so opaque that few, if any, could analyse and value them properly.

The worst part of the structured finance story is that the 1980s vintages of CDO had already proven them to be a poor business model. Investment banks retained the few structured finance deals done in 2008 to collateralise repurchase loans at central banks. They still do not recognise that structured finance is a failed business model and eagerly anticipate the innovation that will thrust it back into the forefront of financing. Hopefully, future structured finance deals will consist of basic, Model T pass-through vehicles that can cause little harm.

The panic phase of the correction in asset prices is over, and a big relief rally in risk assets is in progress. Many investors are eager to participate in this rally, believing it will be the start of a major bull market. It will not be. The necessary restructuring of balance sheets has scarcely begun. It will be a long time before it is completed and the next major bull market can begin. The fluctuations in the real prices of risk assets will basically offset each other until investors give up the hope that the next rally will be the big one. With equity prices trending upward for the last 75 years, that will take a long time.

Borrow-and-spend nations rely on others to do their saving for them – a dangerous practice because a rise in domestic demand abroad could leave them desperately short of saving, especially with soaring government deficits hoovering up savings. The need for growing domestic saving means the downward cycle in interest rates that lasted for 27 years is over and a new structural rise has begun that will last for a similar amount of time. However, like the prices of risk assets, interest rate rises and falls will basically offset each other, so a rising trend will be barely perceptible for the first few years.

Substituting good government debt for bad private debt is lowering the quality of sovereign credit. The final chapter will explore the ramifications of this unprecedented development.

7

Populist policies do not work

B asic factors, such as the long-term trends in demographics, the gravitation of economic activity to emerging nations and the increasing problems in maintaining sufficient supplies of energy, water and food for everyone have constituted a big part of the analysis so far. Important changes, such as the end of the credit cycle, and the rapid growth of government intrusion it fostered, formed another big part. Now it is time to include the impact of society on all the other factors we have discussed.

Governments will grow

Ordinary people are rebelling against being exploited by the privileged. Opposition to governments bailing out the rich at public expense is widespread, causing demonstrations and even rioting in some nations. Mail sent to the US Congress was 99% against government bailouts, yet the Washington–Wall Street Axis (see page 98) has committed vast sums to bailouts, directly contrary to those wishes. A younger cohort of the US population, whose primary concern was to correct the excesses of the Washington–Wall Street Axis over the past 25 years, elected the new administration in the US with a mandate to correct the overly lax regulation on Wall Street. However, governments use economic crises to enlarge their influence, so both government spending and its interference in our daily lives will rise greatly in the next few years.

The Thatcher–Reagan era of limited government, free trade and strong economic growth is history. Strong growth in this era and fiscal multipliers inflated revenues beyond politicians' and bureaucrats' wildest dreams, yet profligate spending led to big deficits in most industrial nations. Then the end of the credit cycle sent asset prices spiralling down, causing an estimated $50 trillion of losses by the end of 2008.

The Fed model of the wealth effect on consumer spending indicates a $1 loss in wealth causes 7½ cents less spending over three years. The Fed calculated that the drop in US household net worth from the first quarter of 2007 to the third quarter of 2008 should reduce consumption by about 3.4% a year from 2009 to 2011 – about 2.4% of GDP. Household net worth has continued to fall since the third quarter of 2008, so this drag on consumer spending will persist into 2012 and most likely beyond. Lower growth from the wealth effect has reversed fiscal multipliers and revenues are dropping sharply, while ageing populations are adding greatly to spending. The additional spending on bank guarantees, fiscal stimulation plans, bailouts and propping up zombie companies is sending fiscal deficits soaring to over double previous record peacetime percentages of GDP.

Reasons for increased fiscal stimulation are dubious

Roberto Perotti, professor of economics at Bocconi University, showed that every borrowed dollar of fiscal stimulus is either irrelevant to GDP or actually shrinks it in the long term. Perotti's paper 'Estimating the effects of fiscal policy in OECD countries', published in 2004,[33] calculated the long-term growth impact of all the stimulus packages of 1% of GDP or more implemented between

1960 and 2000 in the US, Canada, Britain, Germany and Australia. The main conclusions of this study were:

- the effects of fiscal policy on GDP are generally small and tend to be negative;
- tax cuts do not work faster or have higher multipliers than spending increases;
- higher government spending reduces profits and lowers private investment;
- corporations produced better results when governments reduced spending;
- the effects of fiscal policy on GDP have become substantially more negative since 1980.

Other studies support Perotti's work. A National Bureau of Economic Research paper[34] stated that a 10% rise in government spending and taxation reduces output growth by 1.4 percentage points a year, and vice versa. Programmes such as keeping people in unaffordable homes and maintaining zombie companies reduce private investment, which lowers both current and future output.

Unfunded fiscal stimulation programmes obviously add to GDP in the year the government spends the money, but the need to fund the spending or raise taxes impedes growth the next year and every year thereafter for years, if not decades. The US federal deficit will be over 13% of GDP in 2009, more than double the previous peacetime record. The Congressional Budget Office (CBO) estimates the deficit will average about $1 trillion a year from 2010 to 2019 and still be over 5% of GDP at the end of the decade. Worse, taxes will rise sharply.

The liberal consensus is that tax rates do not affect growth or job creation. The Obama budget calls for tax increases of $1.1 trillion over the next decade and 75% of the 'rich' he wants to pay 'their fair share' (i.e. much higher taxes) are small businesses, the creators of the majority of new jobs. Specifically, the Bush tax cuts end in 2010, the expiry of the tax on estates when people die that was scheduled for 2010 has been cancelled, and the tax on cigarettes has been raised by over 150%. The CBO estimates that the European-style cap-and-trade carbon emissions plan (effectively a tax on consumption) will raise revenues by 1.2% of GDP in 2009, 3.2% in 2010 and 4–5% thereafter. Other tax rises, such as the elimination of the tax deferral on international corporate income, will add an additional 2+% of GDP to tax bills over the next couple of years.

Other developed nations have similar problems. For example, the 2009/10 UK budget forecasts deficits of 12.4% of GDP in 2009/10 and 11.9% in 2010/11, gradually declining to zero in fiscal 2017. In addition, taxes will rise by 2.8% of income by 2013/14. These estimates will almost certainly prove to be optimistic. The Institute for Fiscal Studies has estimated it will be two decades before the UK's annual budget deficit drops back to pre-crisis levels.[35]

Government shares of GDP are rising significantly and crowding out the private sector. Fiscal deficits will probably exceed global saving after capital consumption allowances for some time. Quantitative easing will initially fund part of the deficits, but it merely pushes the unfunded borrowing into the future as it must ultimately be funded. As a result, little saving will be available to expand production and raise productivity for a long time. Tax increases scuppered the US recovery in 1936 and the Japanese recovery in 1997, and it will do the same to any future recovery. Tax increases and lack of investment condemn developed nations to slow growth far into the future.

Studies by Christina and David Romer (Christina Romer is chair of Obama's Council of Economic Advisers) show a specific tax rise of 1% of GDP reduces output over the next three years by 3% of GDP as a result of the big impact of tax hikes on saving and private investment.[36] Perotti also showed government spending lowers private investment.[37] The resulting deficits crowd out private investment if governments borrow the needed funds from the private sector and rising inflation misallocates capital if governments monetise the deficits. Also, transferring private debt onto public balance sheets and/or governments recapitalising companies has the same effect as nationalising them. Nationalised companies are notoriously inefficient, so the current bailouts will reduce productivity and living standards.

Governments are emphasising fairness and responsibility in their effort to convince the public that these socialist programmes are necessary moves in the process of restoring growth and creating a fairer society. Capitalism tends to skew rewards to the rich and the more financial activity contributes to total rewards, the greater the skew. Progressive taxation is intended to offset this skew, but it does not. Warren Buffett said his tax rate is half that of his secretary. The rich abusing their privileged status created a strong backlash against the rising disparity in incomes. That backlash swept the US Democrats into power in both houses of Congress and the White House.

The end of the credit cycle will reduce the current overwhelming disparity in incomes and also will increase income mobility. Even so, income disparity will remain a major political issue until the wide income gaps narrow greatly. Governments must curb the excesses of the elite. Moral hazard has pre-empted large amounts of social and financial capital, so the rich are facing much higher tax rates – even though steeper tax gradients reduce investment and so hurt everyone.

If their programmes are to have any chance of success, governments must create enough inflation in prices and incomes to reduce both public and private debt burdens to a tolerable level. Their ability to do so is in doubt. Woody Brock estimates the effect of fiscal stimulus in excess of about 7% of GDP is minimal because excess stimulation causes a steep rise in real, long-term interest rates.[38] As a result, the outsized deficits in the US, the UK and elsewhere are unlikely to stimulate much more output than deficits half their size would have done.

Furthermore, almost five-sixths of the US economy is in the private sector and the government, with its one-sixth share, cannot compensate for the private-sector shrinkage. The government share is bigger in other developed nations, but not big enough bigger to offset private-sector shrinkage – proven by Japan's 'lost decade'. Losses have vaporised so much capital and the private sector is so overindebted that trying to compensate for the destruction of its wealth will trash government balance sheets long before the bailing-out process is complete.

Even if governments do succeed in raising inflation in prices and incomes, they would still have problems. Soaring longer-term interest rates in the first part of 2009 show fixed-income investors realise inflation can accelerate quickly if central banks do not take firm and timely action to prevent it. However, both corporate and household finances are so fragile that relatively small increases in interest rates could multiply default rates. Most people believe corporate balance sheets are stronger than household balance sheets, but corporate defaults quadrupled from 2007 to 2008 (albeit from a low level) and Moody's estimated they would almost quadruple again to 15.1% in 2009[39] – before the rise in interest rates began.

Chapter 3 concluded that inflation is counterproductive, but a possible outcome of the battle between Main Street and the Washington–Wall Street Axis. Main Street controls almost three-quarters of the resources in the US and similar ratios in most other developed nations. Slow to negative growth, low to negative inflation and higher taxes and interest rates will ensure that credit deterioration will continue and offset efforts to stimulate lending and inflation.

The Bank of Japan's quantitative easing did not stimulate inflation, but it also did not double its balance sheet in five years. US and UK quantitative easing more than doubled their balance sheets in a few months, but there is little evidence so far that the outsized effort will be any more effective. Governments probably will have to give up their futile battle against debt liquidation or keep printing unlimited quantities of money and let the government debt-to-GDP ratio spiral out of control. This is the way the US and the UK are heading, and in the past it has always led to an inflationary spiral and a worse crash. Britain is the only nation that tried it with a reserve currency. The Great Depression was the result. Should we expect anything different now from the US?

Dependency on the state is soaring. Both financial and non-financial corporate demands for handouts will keep rising until the zombie companies are put out of their misery. Bank capital will continue to be a black hole until private-sector balance sheets are repaired, Detroit is getting federal funding for its stable of 'green cars' and other companies are lining up for their handouts. A long-run cost of this dependency is an aversion to risk that enervates the entrepreneurial spirit needed for innovation and prosperity. Worse, market-based economies are shifting to political-based ones where the government picks the winners and losers – a job for which it is singularly unqualified.

Moreover, the rich and powerful are acting with complete disdain for the people bailing them out. The recent credit crunch affected developed economies and financial markets in much the same way as the 1929 stock market crash, but the people involved acted very differently. In 1929 people associated with the crash were humbled, humiliated and even jumped out of windows. When the recent credit crunch hit, many of those who were forced out left with golden pay-outs, while others who held onto their jobs were awarded huge bonuses, courtesy of taxpayer-funded bailouts.

Public anger may slim obese governments

Recent events seem to show that the public has become fed up with politicians and bureaucrats rewarding the bad behaviour of the moneyed class, and with rising tax rates while benefits and services, such as pensions, policing and garbage collection, are being cut. The approval ratings of Congress fell from an average of 56% for 2001 to 19% for 2008 and an all-time low of 12% in January 2009. Public anger with politicians is rising in many nations, even staid Britain, where flagrant abuse of politicians' expense allowances has stirred up considerable resentment. This may be the first sign that the public will start to dismiss catchwords and soundbites and insist on results instead. If so, demands for accountability will hopefully force obese governments to slim down. If not, penury will ultimately humble them.

Blanket bank guarantees, recapitalisations, bailouts and spiralling debt-to-GDP ratios are forcing rating agencies to cut the ratings of some sovereign credits and put others on watch for downgrades. The paper presented to the American Economic Association by Reinhart and Rogoff in January 2009[40] shows that government debt in the three years after a banking crisis rises by an average of 86%. The massive fiscal response to the current situation guarantees that not only will the average rise in sovereign debt in borrow-and-spend nations be far more than 86%, but also that the rise will continue far past the three years they studied.

Private debt exceeded its practical limit and caused the credit crunch. Sovereign debt has been modest in many major nations, but that will change in the next decade and we will find the practical limits to sovereign debt too. Supranational agencies have prevented national defaults from causing systemic risk so far, but they have never had to deal with the default of a major nation. We do not know what will happen if a major nation defaults, but we will find out unless all the borrow-and-spend nations institute policies to minimise the growth of government spending and maximise real growth. Policies to minimise government spending would include:

- countercyclical policies expiring automatically with the return of trend growth;

- bringing government accounting up to business standards so investments are properly capitalised and amortised;
- legally binding limits to fiscal deficits and the means to enforce those limits.

Policies to maximise growth would include:

- dedicating the voluntary stimulation to infrastructure investment and stimulating innovation and venture capital;
- rewarding young entrepreneurs and scientific talent from an early age;
- revamping the tax system to reward innovation, investment and success;
- removing corporate regulation where it is not needed and revamping regulation of the financial sector to curtail leverage and improve loan quality;
- deregulating the labour market as to wages and ages.

All these policies would benefit any nation that adopted them. Borrow-and-spend nations are most in need of them but, unfortunately, few if any have adopted even one, so a major nation will suffer a major crisis unless another factor can derail their headlong rushes into potential disaster. Incredibly, the adverse effect of the big deficits on investment should prevent an inflationary spiral, regardless of the amount of fiscal stimulation and quantitative easing.

Governments often spend money badly or provide incentives for others to spend money badly in many more ways than those discussed above. Huge amounts of money are wasted on misguided and badly run procurements – especially on IT and defence programmes. Similarly, big amounts are wasted as a result of pursuing the wrong policy option – perhaps because the government has done insufficient research or because it has been swayed by popular but misinformed opinion.

For example, environmentalism, particularly climate change, has become a major public concern in recent years. Governments have been busy devising policies to combat global warming, but they may not have properly addressed the basic questions of how serious the problem is and what the most effective responses would be. Some experts estimate that the rise in temperature in the next half century will be about 1°C and the average annual rise in the sea level will be little more than the recent average of about 3 millimetres, which should present few problems that could not be controlled or adapted to with forward planning in most places. Moreover, a mild rate of warming would have positive impacts, such as enhanced growth in global vegetation and wildlife and reduced needs for heating in high latitudes. Indeed, climate scientists and policy experts say that nothing we can do to cut emissions will reduce risk from hurricanes or rising seas in the short term, so the best policy is adaptation – building storm surge defences, stopping building in coastal areas and ensuring our fresh-water supplies are protected from salination. Other arguments to do with the causes of melting sea ice, and the important role played by clouds and sunspots, seem to have been similarly underexamined by governments in their policymaking. No ,

Fiscal deficits will crowd out investment

The liberal consensus is that borrowing and spending are essential for output growth and saving subtracts from final demand. It is wrong on both counts. Saving, by definition, transfers spending power to other economic entities that invest it. Saving creates investment, which in turn creates productivity. They were the main factors driving US economic growth from 1949 to 1979; borrowing and spending were the main factors driving it from 1980 onwards. Not only was growth 4% a year in the former period and 2½% in the latter, but borrowing and spending-led growth created a credit bubble that collapsed with serious consequences when the bubble burst.

Credit growth in excess of nominal GDP growth adds nothing to GDP in the long term. It only shifts future GDP to the present. The phrase 'borrowing from the future' says it all. The credit bubble since the credit crunch in the early 1980s borrowed many years of future GDP growth and its collapse into a banking crisis began the payback of all that borrowing. The crash in asset prices vaporised global 'equity' that had been built on printed money rather than saving. This loss of equity is forcing liquidation of the debt financed with printed money and this, in turn, will limit GDP growth until saving funds all the debt outstanding.

Americans, and many others, had believed house prices would rise forever and so do their saving for them. Instead, house prices fell and the unexpected drop in what has proved to be phantom net worth shocked consumers in borrow-and-spend nations (the world's consumers of last resort for a quarter of a century) back into saving mode. For example, Gallup polls showed that people in the US earning over $100,000 reduced their daily spending from $185 in May 2008 to $101 in March 2009. In other words, they have increased their saving by $84 a day.

Even so, US saving in 2008 was less than capital consumption allowances. Depending on imported saving to replace worn-out and obsolete plant and equipment as well as any additions made the US the most saving-deficient major nation in the world. Its borrow-and-spend model is unsustainable in the long run because debt must rise faster than GDP, so borrowers become less creditworthy until the credit bubble bursts, as has just happened. The Chinese save-and-export model is also unsustainable in the long run because over-investment ultimately raises the total risk on the added investment above the potential income, ensuring negative returns, as has just happened.

The private sector in borrow-and-spend nations is saving more but, unfortunately, the big fiscal deficits are more than offsetting domestic saving. Quantitative easing notwithstanding, borrow-and-spend nations will remain dependent on imported saving. The improvement in their trade balances should stop and probably reverse. This is good news for save-and-export nations; their efforts to stimulate their domestic demand have met with little success. Global growth will remain slow and the correction of global savings and investment imbalances will proceed at a snail's pace until their domestic demand increases – probably an extremely long time.

Government efforts to reignite growth, especially quantitative easing, have kindled inflationary fears, but the competition for resources between the public and private sectors that caused soaring inflation in the 1970s will not be a factor in the foreseeable future. Japan's continuing deflation shows not only that private borrowing is an essential part of inflation but also that big rises in the sovereign debt-to-GDP ratio limit output growth for many years.

Low growth and rising tax rates in developed nations mean the private sector will struggle to increase its saving and the fiscal deficits will consume both domestic saving and much, if not all, of the foreign saving imported with current account deficits. Fiscal deficits will crowd out investment for a long time, so the private sector will be unable to compete for resources – precisely what happened throughout the Great Depression. The only nations that will have inflation are those, like Iceland, that also have rapidly falling currencies. Many nations, including the US, are striving to devalue their currencies, so few will succeed in inflating. We will now see how some fundamental changes will affect the economy and financial markets.

Fundamental changes

The collapse of oil prices in 2008 was a big setback for petro-dictators and the big contango in the futures market shows that demand destruction has taken control of oil prices away from OPEC.

POPULIST POLICIES DO NOT WORK

It also shows a general expectation for oil prices to rise in the future. The inability of save-and-export nations to raise domestic demand has ended the world boom, removing any economic reason for oil prices to rise much above the marginal cost of production, which is $50–60 a barrel. No.

Unfortunately, oil and gas prices have been politicised. Recent estimates attribute 63% and 73% of the world's proven oil reserves and gas reserves to Middle East Muslim nations and the former Soviet Union compared with 16%, including the oil sands, and 7% respectively to industrial nations.[41] China and Russia and their allies control a large part of the distribution of oil and gas, so the economic price of oil and gas may become almost meaningless. Industrial nations, which control more than half of the world's coal and uranium reserves, must either revamp their energy policies or depend on potentially unfriendly regimes for oil and gas, thus subjecting themselves to the possibility of price manipulation and shortages.

The great boon of technology has been to reduce the cost of the energy needed to produce each unit of output. Almost all the rise in living standards since the Industrial Revolution has come from reducing the cost of and amount of energy used to produce each unit of output. Energy policies and rising marginal costs of production have raised costs per unit of energy and so ended such gains in developed nations for the foreseeable future.

The relative cost of energy is rising and the gravitation of industrial production to emerging nations has increased the energy input per unit of output. Chapter 1 showed that the relative prices of water and food will rise even if global warming continues – and the benefits of global warming may have ended. These impediments mount a formidable challenge to raising living standards across the world. Overcoming this challenge depends on raising the rate of capital accumulation (saving) sufficiently above the rate of growth of the labour force.

Adding the labour forces of emerging nations to the global pool of productive workers reduced the growth of wages in more developed nations and raised the returns to business assets. Labour's share of national income in developed nations fell to historically low levels and the rise in living standards stalled while profits rose to historically high levels. This, combined with the end of the credit cycle, caused a big shift to the left in politics in some industrial nations. The resulting rise in government funding requirements is counterproductive because it reduces the amount of saving available for the investment needed to improve the ratio of capital accumulation to labour force growth.

Job destruction in the current recession has been greater than in any other recession since the Second World War in many developed nations – even though a highly cyclical industry, manufacturing, has largely moved to emerging nations. Jobs are scarce in big rust belt areas, especially in the US, because emerging nation competition has priced less skilled labour in developed nations out of world markets. Liberal attitudes in developed nations will prevent the nominal price, and probably the real price, of labour from falling to meet the competition. As a result, unemployment will be a continuing problem – even though the growth rate of people of working age is less than 1% and falling, the participation rate in the labour force is falling and immigration is more likely to fall than to rise.

The rising use of energy to replace human effort keeps reducing the need for human work, so the number of hours in a work week keeps falling and the number of days off work in a year keeps rising. Studies show that satisfaction from work is falling and additional leisure time to be with family or pursue other interests is becoming ever more desirable, especially in households where both partners work. Futurists have been talking about a work-free world for over half a century and developed nations now produce enough wealth to allow their citizens to decide how hard they will work – even whether they will work at all.

President Obama supports a basic income guarantee, which

would entitle people who could not find work locally and people who decided not to work to a basic income. America generates enough wealth to fund such a scheme, but an income guarantee would entail a huge transfer of wealth. Its merits and drawbacks will be debated for years, but its implementation seems inevitable. Tax Foundation figures show that 40% of the US population living in income-producing households don't pay federal income tax. In addition, the bottom 50% of all taxpayers paid less than 3% of all income taxes, with an average tax rate of less than 3% – before taking the refundable portion of the Earned Income Tax Credit into account.[42] Thus more than half the voting public are likely to vote for measures that will raise taxes.

Like his idol, Franklin Roosevelt, President Obama is an icon of change. If he is an equally strong leader, the changes will go in the direction he and his supporters want, probably making the US the worst performing major economy in the next decade, as it was in the 1930s. The administration will probably try to paper over this poor performance.

There is also the risk of a lurch into greater protectionism, which may be politically popular but would be economically disastrous, as the Smoot-Hawley tariff proved in the 1930s. Political rhetoric is universally anti-protectionist, but many nations are adopting protection through the back door. Protectionism and other populist policies will minimise growth until significant political reform occurs. However, reform never occurs until the situation has become so bad people that believe anything else would be better. A 60-year boom, the longest and by far the biggest since the flood of gold from the New World in the 16th century, has just ended. It will take some time before people demand reform, but that demand will come.

The automatic stabilisers of the classic gold standard created a faster and more widespread rise in living standards in the 70 years to 1914 than fiat money did after the second world war, because fiat money has an inherent flaw: it depends on those in charge both spotting an unsustainable trend in its infancy and taking the actions required to end it before it has gained too much traction to be reversed. This is a virtually impossible task. So every fiat money system ever tried has ended in disaster. Every fiat money system before the Genoa convention in 1922 was a national, not international, system. The fact that all national systems failed does not mean the current international one will fail too – but it is a warning. Fiat money has resulted in:

- imbalances of global savings and investment rising to untenable levels (see Chapter 2);
- unsustainably low interest rates creating the greatest inflation since the fall of Rome (see Chapter 3);
- excessive leverage causing the biggest credit boom and crash ever (see Chapter 3);
- disruptive capital flows overwhelming perfectly sound fiscal and monetary policies of smaller nations (see Chapter 4);
- government growth soaring and crowding out the private sector.

Fiat money enabled a credit boom that reallocated ever more resources from production to speculation on rising asset prices. The resulting serial asset booms created the highest leverage in history. However, leverage cuts both ways and so destroys as much wealth as it creates. Figures from the Federal Reserve show that US national net worth fell from $80 trillion in the second quarter of 2007 to $65 trillion in the first quarter of 2009. It was not only by far the biggest loss of wealth in the shortest period of time in history, but also the result of many years of quantitative easing, because this had funded the high leverage in the first place.

Central banks resort to quantitative easing because it creates a convincing illusion of rising wealth and so keeps everyone happy in the short term, the only time frame that concerns most people. However, quantitative easing is no substitute for saving. Borrowing saving causes few problems because a solid base exists to accommodate the risks lending and borrowing entail. However, borrowing printed money has no such base and undermines the foundation of the entire asset structure until it ultimately breaks down in a banking crisis. The end of the credit cycle vaporised the part of asset prices based on printed money while the debt remained intact. As a result, net worth fell by the loss in asset prices and severely constrained private-sector ability to borrow. Further quantitative easing will affect the government's ability to repay more than the private sector's.

Quantitative easing allowed the unsustainable imbalances of saving and investment called the Eurasian savings glut to grow and the end of the credit cycle began to correct those imbalances. The optimum economic solution would have been to let the market forces that began the correction finish the job as quickly as possible. However, no regime has dared to try to sell short-term pain as a long-term cure, so governments of both save-and-export and borrow-and-spend nations are doing all they can to resist the correction. Save-and-export nations are failing to stimulate domestic demand; borrow-and-spend nations are not only impeding saving with minuscule interest rates, higher taxes and huge fiscal deficits, but also trying to force banks into perpetuating the credit bubble – while at the same time castigating them for causing it in the first place.

Current policies will minimise output growth and the rise in living standards. Business cycles will continue as before, but recoveries will be shorter and milder, and recessions longer and deeper, than in the past. Average global growth will probably halve from the recent record rates in the next decade. Developed nation growth will probably average 1% a year in the next decade, down from the 2% in the past decade or so. Faster growing emerging nations will probably achieve 4–5% growth, down from 8–10%. The lower rates of growth will ultimately provoke demands for reform, which will include reform of the monetary system.

Forward into the past

Today's floating rate regime was meant to reduce contagion from the dislocations of economic shocks. But as Chapter 4 showed, pro-cyclical international movements of capital can force central banks to lower interest rates in a boom to reduce the inflow when they should be raising them to slow the rate of growth, and to raise interest rates to prevent a capital flight when they should be reducing them to stimulate the economy. Worse, emerging nations incur big risks when they borrow widely accepted currencies in international capital markets because foreign creditors can create a crisis if they fear a default on their loans. Capital flight has caused severe crises in emerging nations across Latin America, in Asia and in eastern Europe in the past two decades.

The monetary policies of emerging nations that borrow foreign currencies must satisfy foreign lenders. Such borrowers gain few benefits, yet can suffer penalties, from conducting their own monetary policy. As a result, some smaller nations that want to borrow in international markets are replacing their currencies with internationally accepted ones. For example, politically volatile Ecuador adopted the US dollar in 2000 and became Latin America's star performer by 2004 with 6.6% real growth and 2.7% inflation, the lowest in 30 years. Such performances will encourage more emerging nations to adopt a major currency as their domestic currency. Could this process continue until only one world currency survived?

A world currency, perhaps based on SDRs as China seems to want, would solve all the foreign exchange problems arising from the existing plethora of about 200 national fiat currencies. However, a world fiat currency would require a global central bank and a global monetary policy. Such a system would retain all the flaws of the current fiat money system yet deprive every nation of an independent monetary policy, an important tool of economic management.

A world monetary policy would usually operate to the detriment of about half the nations in the world. Half the nations in the world may already have detrimental monetary policies, but world co-operation has been a non-starter on far lesser issues. Few major nations would accept such a handicap on such a major policy issue. A global currency also embodies a major disadvantage that currently affects only a few nations.

Sovereign creditors do not default on debt denominated in money they can print. They just reduce benefits and services, as they have done with pensions, policing and garbage collection. However, they do default on debt denominated in money they cannot print. Nations that adopt other currencies as their own cannot print those currencies and so can default on domestic as well as foreign debt. Euro-zone governments cannot print euros, so they too could default on their domestic debt. Worse, the European Central Bank as it is presently set up would charge the losses on the loans it has made against dubious collateral to euro-zone governments, which could force the weakest ones into bankruptcy. Apportioning such losses would be a much greater problem with a global central bank. A world currency would put all nations in the position of euro-zone governments, so sovereign defaults would soar.

Currency reform will probably start with more small nations either adopting a major currency as their own, or creating currency boards. A currency board holds sufficient reserves of the anchor currency to ensure that all holders of the local currency it issues can convert their notes and coins into the anchor currency at the predetermined, fixed exchange rate, with no restrictions on current account or capital account transactions. Currency boards have no powers to regulate banks or influence interest rates and they do not lend to banks or the government.

A fixed peg with a foreign currency has exactly the same effect as adopting that currency. It keeps interest rates and inflation closely aligned to those in the country against whose currency the peg is fixed and so can be a credible commitment to low inflation. It enhances currency stability but removes the ability to set monetary policy according to domestic needs. The fixed exchange rate will also largely fix the nation's terms of trade, irrespective of economic differences between it and its trading partners.

Problems arising from being tied to the flawed monetary policy of a foreign nation will lead to desires for a better system. Currencies that are freely convertible at fixed rates into an asset that can grow only extremely slowly and also constitutes bank reserves would be a better system. It would severely limit growth in total bank reserves. Providing all bank deposits are subject to a reserve requirement, this would remove the ability to inject extra liquidity into the financial system and so limit the growth of the global money supply to non-inflationary levels. Limiting the growth in money supply also limits the total amount of credit that is available. Credit-fuelled booms and the inevitable busts thereafter would be consigned to the dustbin of history.

Free convertibility between currencies and bank reserves makes possible the fixed exchange rates that failed so badly under fiat money because free convertibility activates monetary stabilisers as soon as an imbalance occurs. A current account deficit in excess of the amount foreigners want to invest in that nation reduces its bank reserves, money growth and prices. Lower prices re-establish equilibrium by raising exports and lowering imports. Similarly, a current account surplus in excess of the amount that nation wants to invest abroad raises bank reserves, money growth and prices. Higher prices re-establish equilibrium by lowering exports and raising imports.

As we have seen, the classic gold standard was such a system. It integrated the global economy and financial markets better than fiat money does now. More nations were on the classic gold standard from the 1870s to 1914 than at any other time. Global trade was comparable to today, but purchasing power parities and real interest rates were more equal across the world than before or since.

The monetary stabilisers also prevent destabilising capital flows.

A capital inflow greater than a nation's current account deficit has exactly the same effect as an excessive current account surplus; a capital outflow greater than that nation's current account surplus has exactly the same effect as an excessive current account deficit. Short-term capital flows played a highly stabilising role under the classic gold standard, showing that the monetary system matched available capital to investment needs better than fiat money does now. Modest rises in short-term interest rates reliably stimulated enough short-term capital inflows to finance trade deficits. Crises did occur under the gold standard, but its automatic stabilisers were much more efficient than anything in existence today and recoveries happened sooner and faster.

Gold is the obvious candidate for re-establishing international convertibility because of both its long history and recent trends. Gold is slowly becoming a factor in international trade; Islamic nations are conducting bilateral trade in gold dinars and China has opened a gold exchange. The gold standard optimised growth by creating price stability and keeping interest rates low. Nations normally went on the gold standard to increase their growth rates when they were mired in depressions. The US raised the price of gold to inflate the prices of its goods and services in 1933.

The current monetary system is flawed and will be radically overhauled. Low growth should raise interest in seceding from the euro in the next decade and that should raise interest in currency reform. Worthwhile monetary reform would limit credit growth. That would limit inflation, which in turn would limit government growth, because the fiscal multiplier (see Introduction) makes it the biggest beneficiary of inflation. Obviously, governments would strenuously resist any such monetary reform, so no meaningful change in the monetary system is possible until resentment against falling living standards worsened by continuous tax increases (accompanied by reductions in benefits and services) creates a significant backlash against obese governments.

In short, the world must experience a period of economic hardship before monetary reform is possible but, when it occurs, the reform will help restore optimum growth. Gold is the obvious basis for the new monetary system, but few people believe gold could be monetised. Let us do the maths. Nations and international agencies now own 29,692 tonnes of gold, about 20% of the world's above-ground stock, worth about $750 billion at the May 2009 price of gold of about $950 an ounce. This is far below the CPI-adjusted price of about $2,300 reached in 1980.

The world's broad money supply is about $50 trillion, so a reserve requirement of 5% would require about $2.5 trillion in reserves. Gold monetised at about $3,200 an ounce, 40% more than the real price in 1980, would enable present official holdings to provide adequate reserves for the world's current money supply. This appears reasonable, as Roosevelt raised the gold price by 65% in 1933. Deflation will limit the future growth in money stocks. Some central banks are raising their gold reserves and others are talking about it.

Furthermore, gold will be monetised at a price well above the then market price as a reflationary measure, so current reserves are adequate to reinstate the classic gold standard. A 5% gold reserve requirement on all bank deposits and bank borrowing would automatically limit bank leverage to 20 times net tangible equity, the leverage limit that kept Canadian banks safe in the recent meltdown.

Conclusion

In the early days of model building, an astute econometrician quipped, 'If we knew enough to input our models accurately, we wouldn't need the models.' A model's accuracy depends on the underlying assumptions incorporated into it. An underlying assumption incorporated into all models is that responses to conditions and policies will be the same as in the past. This belief is wrong, so all model-based forecasts are suspect. Leading indicators predicted output growth well until the 1990s, but considerably less well thereafter. Similarly, monetarist models began giving ever less accurate forecasts and the close relationship between interest rates and equity markets broke down after the credit crunch. Economies are not responding as they did in the past, so new forecasting techniques are needed.

Moreover, projecting the present into the indefinite future is futile. Who in 1982 forecast that the Dow Jones Industrials, which had fallen to well under 1,000, would exceed 10,000 by the turn of the century? Similarly, who in 2001 predicted that copper, which had fallen to $0.60 a pound, would trade at $4 in 2006? Change happens faster than anyone believes it can because perceptions lag behind events. Few people have yet recognised that the end of the credit cycle has ended the post-war series of credit-fuelled booms. No amount of quantitative easing and fiscal stimulation will stimulate another. Deflation will change conditions and public attitudes much more quickly than people would believe possible now.

Chapter 4 showed that fiat money ended reversion to the mean. Conditions and markets now go to one extreme and then reverse and go to the other extreme. Periods of poor returns follow periods of outsized returns as reliably as night follows day. Governments and the financial community are counting on the Keynesian theory that government spending compensating for deficient private spending has a multiplier effect that restores prosperity without anyone having to do anything. Reality does not work that way. Empirical evidence shows that an added dollar of government spending adds less than a dollar to GDP in the short term and virtually nothing over the long term. Worse, the short-term effect of each unit of fiscal stimulus diminishes as the total amount increases. Raising output is best left to the private sector.

Free markets have greatly exceeded public-sector ability to create jobs and prosperity, so the continuing intrusion of big government will cost jobs and reverse the rise in living standards. Developed nation governments face the perfect fiscal storm of rising costs, falling income and soaring debt-to-GDP ratios. Pain is inevitable, but more than six decades of unparalleled prosperity have imbued belief that the process of wealth creation carries on automatically, so prosperity is everyone's birthright and no one should be allowed to take it away from them. That belief is stimulating resistance to bailing out the rich. The resistance is already causing angry demonstrations in some nations.

The demonstrations are warranted. The rich and powerful profited greatly from the rising leverage in the serial asset bubbles. The rest of the population did not. The bubbles burst and the high leverage not only reversed the big profits, but also threatened the solvency of a big part of the financial industry. It contributes a big part of the funding for election campaigns, so politicians have concocted arguments for bailing it out even though it does not deserve this largesse. Some governments have passed laws to limit abuses by those that have been bailed out, but market forces will do a much better job of rebalancing the economy than any government could ever hope to do.

For example, the financial industry outgrew its usefulness as private credit growth soared to unsustainable levels. The lower rates of credit growth and return on capital can no longer support the high costs of the financial industry in its glory days. It is now in the early stages of drastic reform – demonstrated by all five leading US investment banks becoming part of the regulated banking system in 2008. Unfortunately, governments will pile on a lot of counterproductive regulations that are unlikely to include the one absolutely essential regulation – universal limits on leverage. Tightening limits on leverage when the rate of credit growth is rising and relaxing them when the rate of credit growth is falling would be an ideal countercyclical measure – and one that would ensure the safety of the banking system.

Figure 7.1 **Estimated world population, 0–2000 (in billions)**

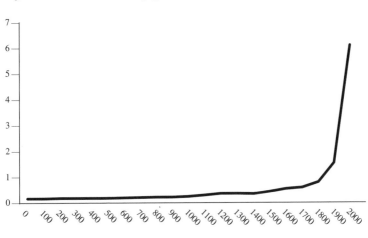

Source: United Nations

The end of the credit cycle is forcing consumers to retrench. Borrowing ourselves out of debt, which most governments are trying to promote, is the height of folly. Higher saving is essential to enable the repair of balance sheets with the minimum of distress. The rise in savings rates indicates that the public is becoming more conservative, which should ultimately trigger a grassroots revolt against obese government that will usher in the reforms needed to underpin a new period of prosperity.

The ageing of populations is reducing the growth rate of the global labour force and some national labour forces are now stable to shrinking. Slimming obese government will enable the rate of capital accumulation to exceed the growth rate of the labour force enough to raise the standard of living for most workers. Indeed, if the rate of innovation is high enough, a global shortage of labour could emerge in the 2030s, in which case living standards would rise rapidly – with one major precondition.

Figure 7.2 **Estimated world population, 1900–2050 (in billions)**

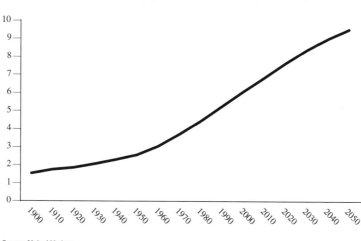

Source: United Nations

Figure 7.1 shows estimated world population in the Common Era to 2000. Growth was imperceptible for the first 900 years at 0.03% a year. It trebled to 0.09% a year in the next 500 years, as a result of the medieval warming period. It trebled again to 0.29% a year in the following 350 years to the early Industrial Revolution in 1750. The rate of growth doubled to 0.6% a year in the next 150 years, which brings us to the beginning of the 20th century when the world population was about 1.5 billion. The rate of growth more than doubled in the 20th century to 1.38% a year, bringing the population to over 6 billion at the start of the 21st century. The global population has now passed 6.7 billion, having grown more in seven years than in the first 1750 years of the Common Era.

Figure 7.2 shows the remarkable explosion in world population in the 20th century. Fortunately, the rate of growth had peaked by 1970 and has been falling ever since. Even so, the current rate of growth of about 1¼% is still high, having never been reached prior to the 1950s. The UN forecasts that population growth will keep falling,[40] yet the global population will rise to over 9 billion in 2050. Extrapolating the UN figures gives a peak population in 2070 of 9.5 billion and a decline thereafter.

The remarkable rise in population growth was possible because the higher productivity from the improving technology of the Industrial Revolution raised agricultural output far faster than any other industry's. Increasing food production had not only already begun to raise population growth significantly by 1798 when Thomas Malthus predicted the global population would outrun the food supply in the middle of the 19th century, but also enabled ever rising population growth into the second half of the 20th century.

The rising food and energy costs described in Chapter 1 and the continuing rise in population for another 60-odd years raise two critical questions:

- Will there be enough fresh water to support the growing population?
- Can the world keep producing ever higher global living standards as the real costs of water, food and energy rise?

The population explosion is exerting ever more severe pressure on a diminishing global supply of potable water. Potable water has no substitute and no big new supply will be discovered. Improving the infrastructure – such as capturing rainwater, reusing grey water, fixing leaks and desalination – can probably augment natural supplies enough to satisfy the 30% of the total demand for water that comes from residential, commercial and industrial sources, albeit at much higher prices. However, disappearing lakes, falling river flows and shrinking aquifers show that the infrastructure is failing to satisfy the 70% of total demand for agricultural use. Worse, the glaciers that feed many major rivers are disappearing at an increasing rate. Indian climate experts have warned that Himalayan glaciers may disappear completely by 2035.

The simple equation, water = food, will ultimately restrict the total population the world can sustain. No one has ever estimated what that limit may be or when it may occur, so there is no guarantee we have not already passed that limit without realising we have done so. Maintaining adequate supplies of water and food will pose far more serious problems than global warming, or even the end of the credit bubble, yet neither water nor food occupy a significant place in the public consciousness. The notion that rising prosperity is the birthright of everyone will fade as the effort to provide everyone with the necessities of life increases.

Solving the rising problems of providing adequate supplies of food and water to everyone will take leadership with foresight, a quality that has been in rather short supply recently. Unrestrained growth in all directions is no longer a viable option, so while we may continue to charge headlong into the future, we can no longer count on others to save us from our excesses. A Chinese proverb says, 'If we do not change the direction we are headed, we will end up where we are going.' Where we are going is not somewhere most of us want to be. We are capable of changing direction, but are we wise enough to do so?

TEN BASIC TRUTHS

1	Fiat money has proven irresistible to governments across the centuries because it permits them to inflate with money central banks print.
2	Printed money = excessive borrowing = the illusion of rising wealth.
3	Illusory wealth ends up in bankruptcy, risk aversion and deflation.
4	Efforts to re-inflate create moral hazard and subsidise the rich at the expense of the poor.
5	We can't borrow our way out of debt.
6	Ageing populations = slow growth = a protracted adjustment.
7	The surplus of workers in emerging nations limits income growth.
8	Creating real wealth requires using savings efficiently.
9	The classic gold standard's automatic stabilisers create sustainable growth.
10	All previous fiat money systems have ended in disaster.

Notes

1 Will Hutton, 'Britain would benefit from Clinton's tough love', *The Observer*, 3 September 2006.

2 'European public spending', *Financial Times*, p. 18, 2 May 2006.

3 Robert Bothwell, Ian Drummond and John English, *Canada Since 1945: Power Politics and Provincialism*, University of Toronto Press, 1981, p. 32.

4 'Canada should seize the challenge of clean coal', *Globe and Mail*, 16 May 2007.

5 BBC2, 'Nuclear Nightmares', broadcast 13 July 2006. The programme gave figures only for deaths caused by the Chernobyl explosion, not for illness and disability.

6 'Skyward oil stokes a coal fired future', *Globe and Mail*, 18 July 2008.

7 'Planet friendliness in China and the USA', The Skeptical Optimist, http://boomerang.blogs.com/optimist/2007/03/planetfriendlin.html (accessed May 2009).

8 *Market Focus*, Credit Suisse, 17 July 2008.

9 US Water News, www.uswaternews.com/archives/ arcconserv/7shanmayx2.html (accessed April 2009).

10 'From Inside China', http://www.pbs.org/kqed/chinainside/nature/ greengdp.html.

11 'Price of water rising', Peopleandplanet.net, 8 March 2007.

12 For a more comprehensive and well-documented description of water shortages and their effect on agriculture see: Lester Brown, *Plan B*

2.0: Rescuing a Planet Under Stress and a Civilization in Trouble, revised edn, W.W. Norton, 2006, Chapter 3.

13 *World Trade Report 2008–2009*, World Health Organisation.

14 Reported in the *Guardian* ('Islamophobia worse in America now than after 9/11'), 10 March 2006.

15 Phillip Longman, *The Empty Cradle*, Basic Books, 2004, p. 54.

16 Hudson & Den Boer, 'A Surplus of Men, a Deficit of Peace: Sex and Security in Asia's Largest States', www.stlawu.edu/gov/361F02Hudson.html (accessed December 2008).

17 Longman, *op. cit.*

18 'Measuring worth purchasing power of British pounds from 1264 to 2007', Institute for the Measurement of Worth, www.eh.net/hmit/ppowerbp (accessed January 2009).

19 'Measuring worth purchasing power of money in the United States from 1774 to 2007', Institute for the Measurement of Worth, www.eh.net/hmit/ppowerusd (accessed January 2009).

20 Federal Reserve Bank of Dallas, 'Making sense of the economic slowdown', Economic Letter, Vol. 1, No. 11, November 2006.

21 Mortgage figures from RealtyTrac press release, 14 January 2009.

22 'More mortgage borrowers going underwater', *USA Today*, 4 March 2009.

23 Martin S. Feldstein, 'Inflation, capital taxation, and monetary policy', National Bureau of Economic Research, Working Paper no. 680, April 1985.

24 Erica Lynne Goshen and Mark E. Schweitzer, 'The effects of inflation on wage adjustments in firm-level data: grease or sand?', working paper no. 9418, Federal Reserve Bank of Cleveland, January 1996.

25 'A brief discussion of earnings and other fundamentals', Decision Point, www.decisionpoint.com/tacourse/Earnings.html (accessed May 2009).

26 Michael Lewitt, 'How to fix it', *The HCM Market Letter*, 1 April 2008.

27 'Five emerging trends will reshape global banking in next decade', IBM press release, 15 November 2005.

28 'Foreclosure update: over 8 million foreclosures expected', Credit Suisse, 4 December 2008.

29 Remarks by John C. Dugan, US Comptroller of the Currency, before the third annual national housing forum, 8 December 2008.

30 www.forbes.com/2009/05/14/taxes-social-security-opinions-columnists-medicare.html (accessed May 2009).

31 Professor Robert W. Holthousen, The Wharton School of the University of Pennsylvania, www.execed-web.wharton.upenn.edu/course.cfm?Program=MA (accessed February 2009).

32 Rob Arnott Research Affiliates, 'Rethinking fixed income', *Journal of Indexes*, May/June 2009.

33 Roberto Perrotti, 'Estimating the effects of fiscal policy in OECD countries', October 2004. This article has been published in many different places over a number of years.

34 Anne O. Krueger, 'Impact of government on growth and trade', National Bureau of Economic Research, Working Paper no. 3545, December 1990.

35 David Smith, 'IMF gloomy – IFS warns of a long road ahead', David Smiths EconomicsUK.com, 29 January 2009.

36 Christina and David Romer, 'The macroeconomic effects of tax changes: estimates based on a new measure of fiscal shocks', National Bureau of Economic Research, Working Paper no. 13264, July 2007.

37 Perrotti, *op. cit.*

38 Woody Brock, 'The end game draws nigh – the future evolution of the debt-to-GDP ratio', on John Mauldin's 'Outside the Box', 18 May 2009.

39 'Credit conditions deteriorate further', *Corporate Financier*, March 2009.

40 Carmen M. Reinhart and Kenneth S. Rogoff, 'The aftermath of financial crises', National Bureau of Economic Research, Working Paper no. 14656, January 2009.

41 PennWell Corporation, *Oil and Gas Journal*, Vol. 106, No. 48, 22 December 2008.

42 Gerald Prante, 'Summary of latest federal individual income tax data', Tax Foundation, 30 July 2009.

Index